KEY TO SIOUX SYMBOLS

1. *Wapa Hasapa*—War bonnet, Authority
2. *Marpiya Wakankdi*—Mysteries of Heaven
3. *Pte He Karpa*—Buffalo skull, Life
4. *Wicarpi*—Star
5. *T'ate Wicoti*—Camp of enemy buffalo hunters
6. *Wa*—Snowflake
7. *Tahohmun-ohmun*—Track in new snow
8. *Tatanka oye*—Buffalo track, sign of plenty, Feasting
9. *Hogan Huhu*—Fishbones
10. *Ziktana*—Flight of birds
11. *Zitka oye*—Bird tracks
12. *Mato oye*—Bear tracks
13. *Kimimi*—Butterfly, Joy

Legends
of the
Mighty Sioux

They lived a happy life

Legends of the Mighty Sioux

Compiled by
WORKERS OF THE SOUTH DAKOTA WRITERS' PROJECT
WORK PROJECTS ADMINISTRATION

Writers' Program – South Dakota

Illustrated by
SIOUX INDIAN ARTISTS

j 398.2
W93

ALBERT WHITMAN & COMPANY
CHICAGO   ILLINOIS

1941

FEDERAL WORKS AGENCY
John M. Carmody, *Administrator*

WORK PROJECTS ADMINISTRATION
Howard O. Hunter, *Acting Commissioner*
Florence Kerr, *Assistant Commissioner*
M. A. Kennedy, *State Administrator*

The Young Citizen of the
South Dakota Department of Public Instruction
Cooperating Sponsor
University of South Dakota
Official Sponsor

Copyright, 1941, by
SOUTH DAKOTA DEPARTMENT OF PUBLIC INSTRUCTION
Printed in the U. S. A.

Preface

The Sioux Indians have given up many of their old dances and have discarded their war spears, but they still continue to observe the old custom of storytelling. Their legends cling to them as closely as their scalp-locks.

While this is neither the first nor the last publication on the subject, an attempt is made here to present a collection of the most interesting and most important stories that are being told among the Mighty Sioux. In editing the book, I had a vast amount of material, gathered by myself and Indian workers of the South Dakota Writers' Project, from which to choose. Many of the stories were told by very old men who never learned to speak English. In the Indian tongue, for instance, old Tasonkesapa told me "The Story of a Hard Winter" which he had often heard told by his grandfather. As we sat in the shade of the trees along the banks of Pickerel Lake, Tasonkesapa closed his eyes while he began to talk, and as he recalled the legend his words came faster, his hands moved deftly to illustrate the story, and his eyes grew bright with excitement. When he had finished, we smoked his pipe. I told him that I would like to give him a present. He looked pleased, and nodded toward my tennis shoes. I took them off, and the last time I saw Tasonkesapa he was still wearing them. To those persons interested in reading Sioux lore, the Writers' Project offers this book; to those who wish to hear legends firsthand, an interpreter and a pair of spare shoes will be helpful.

Grover Horned Antelope, Vonette Rud, and Noah Jumping Elk—pupils in rural elementary schools—suggested many of the pictures. Oscar Howe, Indian artist of the South Dakota Art Project, re-drew the pictures and made the designs.

Credit for valuable assistance is due to members of the Rosebud Sioux Tribal Council, who read the material and endorsed the book; the Bureau of Ethnology, Smithsonian Institution; Dr. E. C. Ehrensperger of the University of South Dakota; and Lora Crouch, Librarian, Mitchell Public Library. We are especially indebted to Mrs. Hazel V. Peterson, Elementary School Supervisor, and Miss Cordelia Shevling, editor of *The Young Citizen,* both of the South Dakota Department of Public Instruction, who gave generous help without which the book could not have been produced.

MONTANA LISLE REESE
State Supervisor
South Dakota Writers' Project

Contents

	PAGE
THE MIGHTY SIOUX	15
The Land of the Sioux	17
The Life of the Sioux	23
Sioux Boys and Girls	31
Songs and Stories	36
TRADITIONAL LORE	43
How the Sioux Nation Was Born	45
The Birth of a Tribe	47
The Gift of the Peace Pipe	49
How the Two Kettle Band Was Named	52
Burnt Hip	54
The Owl's Warning	57
The Snail and the Beaver	62
How the Rainbow Came to Be	64
Why the Baby Deer Wears Spots	67
How Ducks Got Their Colors	69
Why the Leaves Fall	71
CAMPFIRE TALES	75
The Story of a Hard Winter	77
Iktomi Seeks a Bride	86
Beaver Image	90
Fleetfoot	93
Putting the Bee on Bruin	95
The Sun Gazer	97

CONTENTS—Cont'd

	PAGE
The Hunter and the Wolf	101
The Woman and the Wolves	103
The End of the World	105

LEGENDS OF PLACES 107
- The Black Hills 109
- The Vision of Bear Butte 111
- The Guardian of the Pools 113
- How Devil's Tower Came to Be 115
- How Enemy Swim Lake Was Named 117
- Punished Woman's Lake 120
- Maiden's Isle 123
- Lake of the Big Lodge 125
- The Sack of Gold at Long Lake 126
- The Story of Standing Rock 128
- How Snake Butte Was Named 130
- The Naming of White River and the Badlands 132

HUNTING AND BATTLE STORIES 135
- A Boy Becomes a Warrior 137
- The Hunter Rides a Buffalo 139
- A Buffalo Hunter's Escape 141
- The Story of the Screaming Ghost 143
- A Run for His Life 148
- The Battalion of Death 150
- The Scout Who Stopped a War 152
- The Fool Soldiers Band 155
- Sitting Bull's Dancing Horse 157

LIST OF ILLUSTRATIONS

PAGE

They lived a happy life.................Frontispiece

They spend their time out-of-doors.............. 25

The native dances are still seen at powwows....... 39

Swan saw the face of an enemy looking down..... 59

In the sky are all the flowers.................... 65

The trees take on their farewell colors........... 73

The Sunflower's face is ever turned toward the sun. 99

1. The Mighty Sioux

THE LAND OF THE SIOUX

THE Sioux Indians were great hunters and warriors. Buffalo meat, wild fruit, and vegetables made them strong. Hunting made them brave and adventurous. Keeping enemy tribes out of their home lands made them fine fighters. The Sioux warriors were famous for their bravery, and their laws for clean living were very strict.

Tribes of the great Sioux Nation liked so much to hunt that many years ago they chased out all other Indian tribes from the country where the herds of wild buffalo lived. The Mighty Sioux, as they were called by their enemies, took over as their own all the land that is now South Dakota, and parts of North Dakota, Minnesota, Wyoming, Nebraska, and Montana.

The land of the Sioux Nation was so large that each of the Sioux tribes picked out a region of its own in which to live. Those who lived among the lakes and trees of western Minnesota and eastern South Dakota were people of the Sisseton (sis'y-ton), Wahpeton (wa'-pe-ton), Mdewakanton (dē-wa'kon-ton), and Santee (san-tē) tribes of Sioux Indians. Between them and the Missouri River were the Yankton, Upper Yanktonnais (yank-ton-ā'), and Hunkpatina (hunk-pä-tē'nä) tribes.

Farther west, on the rolling plains and in the Black Hills, lived the large Teton (tē'tŏn) division which included such tribes as the Ogallala (ōg"a-lä'la), Rosebud, Two Kettle, Hunkpapa (hunk-pa'pa), Upper and Lower Brule (brū'lē), Sansarc (san'zark), Blackfoot, and Minniconjou (min"i-kon'jū).

These names sound strange, but each had a certain meaning to describe where the tribes lived. The Indian word "Wahpeton" means Village among the Leaves because people of this tribe lived where there were many lakes and trees. "Teton" is the Indian way of saying "dwellers on the prairie" for these people spent most of their time hunting buffalo where they could see for long distances.

In each tribe there were usually several bands or camps named for the chief of the village. That is why one hears of the Drifting Goose Band, or the Red Cloud Band of the Ogallala Tribe.

When the early explorers and missionaries visited the Sioux Nation, they found about 25,000 Sioux Indians living there. Nowadays one does not see many Indians, but it is surprising to know that there are more Indians in South Dakota now than there were before any white men lived in this region. Most Indians now live on reservations—large tracts of land set aside for them.

Although the Sioux kept all other Indian tribes out of their hunting ground, they quickly made friends with the white explorers. The Indians traded buffalo skins and fast horses for guns and pretty beads. To show their desire to be friends with the white men, Sioux leaders signed a treaty promising "peace and friendship forever" with the United States. The chiefs could not write as we do, so they dipped fingers in their own blood and made thumb prints on the paper. This treaty, worn with age, is still kept by Indian great-grandsons in a bank in Sioux Falls, South Dakota.

Peace continued until farmers moved into the Indian country. Soon the white men built fences around groves of wild fruit trees, and the wild animals were frightened away. Then other white men discovered gold in the Black Hills and built trails through the Indian Country to the mountains which were a sacred meeting place of the Sioux. Towns grew up where the Sioux liked to camp and hunt.

The Mighty Sioux no longer had a place of their own. They liked to be free. They wanted to hunt and to live as they pleased, but here were the white people taking away their land, their hunting, and their fun.

So the Mighty Sioux went on the warpath. They chased out settlers and drove back the United States soldiers who came to stop them. More troops of our Army were sent to Dakota, the land of the Sioux. But the Sioux had some great chiefs and were not easily defeated. Sitting Bull, Rain-In-The-Face, Red Cloud, Crazy Horse, Gall, Spotted Tail, and American Horse —all great men and brave leaders—led swift attacks. The fighting grew fiercer. The troops of General George A. Custer were trapped by the crafty Sioux, and every white man killed.

The United States soldiers were smart fighters. Before long they divided the Sioux tribes, and conquered each one. When the battles ended, the Sioux chiefs said they wanted to be brothers with the white men.

Again there were more treaties. The Indians agreed to live on the reservations, away from the white people. In return, the Government gave them clothing, wagons, and cows. This meant that the Mighty Sioux were no longer to be hunters and warriors, but instead they were to become farmers and homebodies. The Government has now built fine schools and hospitals to educate and take care of them.

Many Indian families still live in tents and log houses. A few have good houses and live like white people. Some of the Sioux are good farmers and ranchers. Others work for the Government in building roads and forming lakes. They still hold their tribal councils and have Indian courts to punish lawbreakers. Powwows, where they dance and sing as in the olden days, are held often in summer, and rodeos are very popular.

The Sioux Indians nowadays may be visited on any of the nine reservations in South Dakota. The reservations bear Indian names, and on some of them the Indians live much as they used to do years ago. The reservations are Cheyenne River, Crow Creek, Flandreau,

Lower Brule, Pine Ridge, Rosebud, Sisseton, Standing Rock, and Yankton.

The Sioux people are very fond of all children. Chiefs of the Mighty Sioux are happy to have their pictures taken with white children. Visitors to a reservation will find that the Indian people are very friendly.

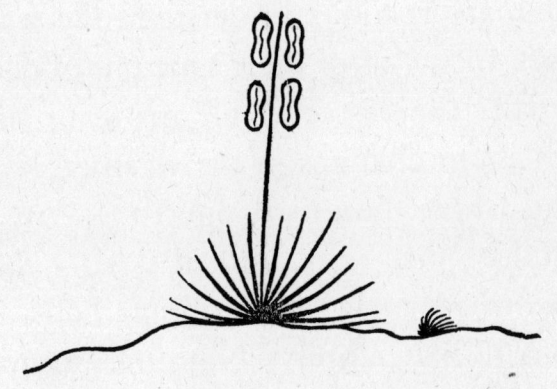

THE LIFE OF THE SIOUX

The Sioux bands once lived a happy, roving life. They followed the great herds of buffalo because these animals were the source of their food supply. They also moved often while making raids on enemy tribes, and to find better places to camp.

It is true that the Sioux understand the ways of Nature, for they spend all of their time out-of-doors. From birds, animals, flowers, and all growing things they learn to tell about changes in the weather, how to keep healthy, and where there is danger.

The buffaloes that were hunted during the summer and fall furnished many of the things that were needed for the Sioux to live happily. Nothing was ever wasted. The meat that was not cooked right away was hung out in the sun to dry. This sun-cured meat was packed away for use while traveling or for the winter's supply. Bones were used to make lard for cooking and for greasing the hair. Some of the soft bones from young animals were used to make cooking utensils and war implements. The skins were used to make teepees, clothing, and warm, heavy robes. It was a law among the Sioux never to kill more buffaloes than were needed.

While following the buffaloes or making enemy raids, a large village that was at Enemy Swim Lake one day might be found many miles away in Long Hollow the next day. When a camp was to be moved, the women skillfully took down the teepees within a few minutes. They packed each teepee in a bundle and tied it, together with the poles, on a pony. Other belongings and small children were placed in a travois which was made like a stretcher and dragged behind the pony.

Camp sites were usually chosen beside lakes or streams where there were hills and trees to protect the village from being seen by enemy scouts. If wild game and berries were plentiful, the band might stay in one location for two or three months. Sometimes camps were moved nearly every day. When the wind grew cold and snow began to fall, the Indians looked for valleys and forests for their camps. Snow fences were built on the north side of each teepee, and enough firewood was gathered to last all winter.

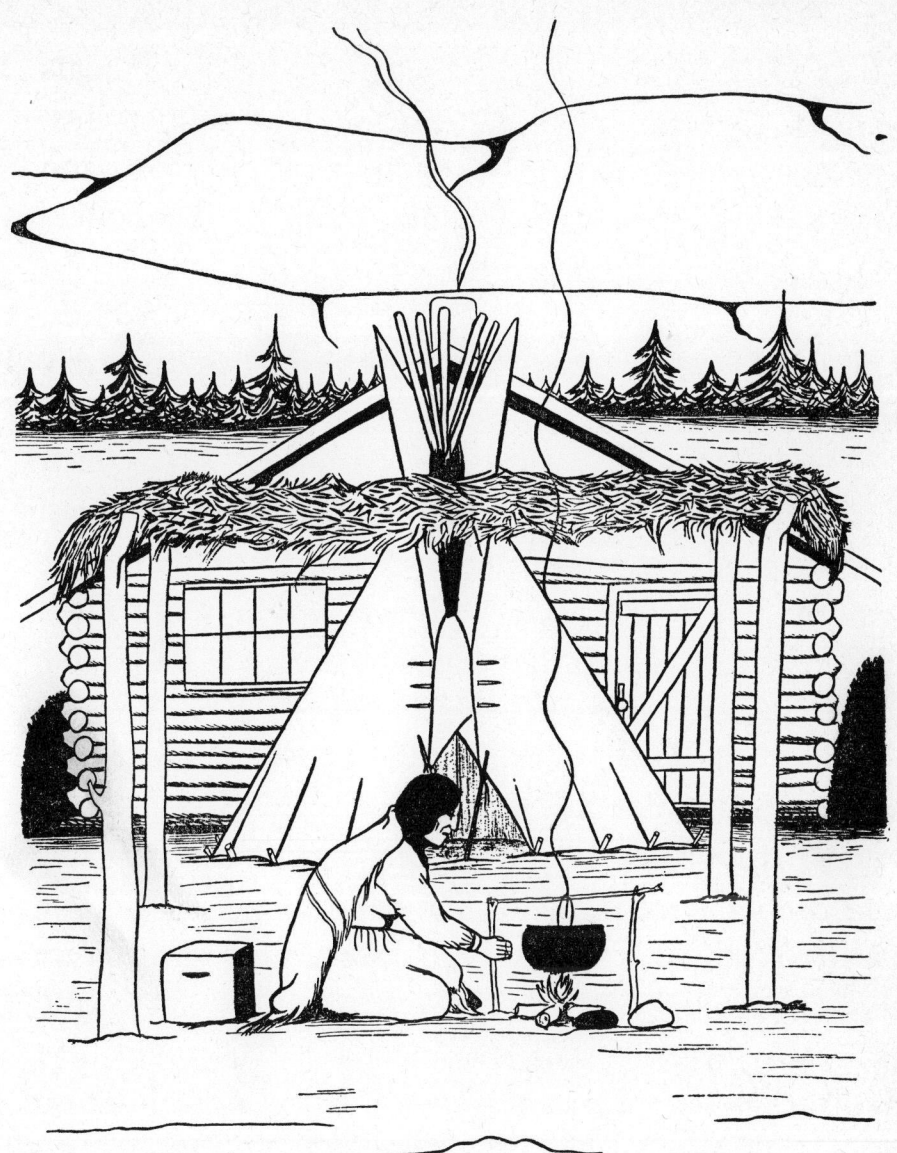

They spend their time out-of-doors.

On special occasions there were council fires, ceremonies, and powwows.

Nowadays when a mother wants to please her family, she bakes a blueberry pie or orders a quart of chocolate ice cream, but when an Indian woman gave her family a special treat it was a food called *wasna*. It was, and still is, a prized kind of cake made by mixing ground meat and wild berries.

Other foods eaten by the Sioux included wild rice, beans, turnips, cactus buttons, buffalo berries, wild grapes, rose berries, willow buds, chokecherries, and gooseberries. In some villages squaw corn was grown and dried for winter eating. Fresh bird's eggs were served in the spring as a special dish. Fish, caught with a hook made from the rib of a mouse, were popular too.

Herbs and roots were used as medicine to cure various illnesses. These were usually prepared by the Medicine Man who, like the Chief of the village, was highly respected. He was also feared for his powers in healing the sick and foretelling events. Besides serving as a doctor, the Medicine Man had charge of all holy ceremonies, interpreted dreams and signs, and helped to make plans for war parties. Sitting Bull was one of the best known of Sioux Medicine Men.

If Sioux warriors still dressed as they used to, they would probably be arrested, for the men usually were dressed only in breech clouts — a strip of buckskin around the hips and between the legs.

Sioux women, in the old days, did not dress very much as women do nowadays either. They wore long buckskin dresses over high leggings, and often they had blankets over their heads or shoulders. On special occasions men wore feathered headdresses, decorated war shirts, bracelets, necklaces, claws, and animal tails. Faces were greased and painted in bright colors, and earrings were made of pretty stones or shells. Elk teeth, porcupine quills, and paints were used to decorate clothing, and after the early traders brought bright-colored beads, these became very popular, especially on moccasins.

Paints were made from soil, rocks, vegetables, and fruits. For instance, black was made from burnt ash wood, and white was ground from light limestone. When some important event happened to a family, a picture of it was often painted on the teepee.

Since the Indians had no calendars as we know them now, they counted years by the number of winters. Their record was known as a Winter Count. The most important thing that happened during the year was painted in colors on a buffalo hide. From these winter counts much of the history of Sioux bands has been learned.

The Big Missouri Winter Count, kept by a family of Rosebud Sioux, was begun while George Washington was President of the United States. The first picture drawn on the Winter Count is for the year 1796. It shows two sets of hoof marks, three on each side, pointing toward each other. The meaning of the picture is interpreted like this: "This is the winter known as the winter of horse-stealing camp because two enemy camps were close to each other. A very deep snow fell and neither camp was able to move, so during the winter each camp stole horses from the other."

One of the last pictures on the hide shows an Indian and a white man at each end of a large bridge crossing a river. This is interpreted to mean that in this year (1925) a bridge was built across the Missouri River connecting the Rosebud country with the eastern part of the State of South Dakota. The Big Missouri's Winter Count is now the property of the U. S. Office of Indian Affairs, and can be seen at the City Museum in Rapid City, South Dakota.

Just as the Sioux counted years by the winters, so they

counted months by each full moon. If an Indian said that a baby was born during "the moon when chokecherries are ripe," he would mean July. Each moon had a certain name. If a boy bought a new bicycle in December, to an old Indian the purchase would mean "the moon when the deer shed their horns." When a hunter went on a journey he did not say that he would be gone for so many days, but for so many "sleeps."

Like the wild buffalo, most of the old Sioux customs and traditions have disappeared. Today the life of the Sioux people is bound closely to the patterns of their white neighbors. Only the very old men and women can recall the days when the Sioux tribes ruled the Dakota plains.

SIOUX BOYS AND GIRLS

A BOY who was born in an Indian family might have been called Buffalo-Lies-On-The-Ground or Pretty Horse Face. Most Indian children were named for some animal, bird, or object that had some special importance to the family. To be named Pretty Horse Face, for example, was a compliment because it means that either the child or the father had a fine horse with a handsome face.

Until recent years the names of one family were usually all different. Chief Iron Shell's seven sons were Hollow Horn Bear, Goes to War, Brave Bird, Swimming Skunk, Little Iron Shell, Holy Man, and Bear Dog. Women's names usually ended in *win,* a Sioux word for woman. So Wanbli win was Eagle woman, and Pte-san win was White Buffalo woman.

In the olden days, when children grew to manhood,

their names were changed as the result of some brave deed. Chief Two Strikes of the Brule Sioux was known as White Bear until he tomahawked two Pawnees who were riding the same horse during a battle. Chief Standing Bear, the Indian writer, says his name as a child was Plenty Kill. Sitting Bull was named Jumping Badger before he became famous.

Today Indian children must be given their father's family name, the same as in white families. Many first names for Sioux children are taken from the Bible, and on the reservations there are many boys and girls with such names as Joseph Blue Dog, Joshua Comes Out, Mary Afraid of Horses, and Sarah Never Miss A Shot.

Until the white men took over the Sioux country, Indian boys and girls did not go to school. Instead, the boys lived a free life, learning to ride, shoot, and hunt. Young girls spent most of their time with their mothers, learning to sew and cook.

Between the ages of six and nine years, boys learned to use the bow and arrow. At first they used arrows that had blunt points, and by the time a boy was ten or eleven years old he could shoot well enough so that he was taken on buffalo hunts.

Boys wore loose buckskin shirts that hung down be-

Sioux Boys and Girls 33

low the knees, and a pair of moccasins. Girls wore buckskin dresses that came to their ankles. Underclothing was seldom worn and children slept in their clothes. It was an unwritten rule of the Sioux tribes that all young boys and girls go to bed when the sun went down and be among the first to greet the rising sun in the morning.

After breakfast, which often was a bowl of soup and boiled beef, the boys hunted wild birds and squirrels, and played such games as leap frog, crack the whip, or held foot races. While the boys were hunting and playing, the girls played with dolls of buckskin and beads, and went swimming with other girls and older sisters. For boys, errands such as inviting some neighbor to the lodge, driving the family herd to water, or gathering dry sticks, took up part of a typical day. Girls were assigned to tasks such as sewing designs and pounding berries.

Many days were spent riding young colts, for each Indian boy trained his own pony for future use.

Camps were often made along creeks, so water games and swimming were popular sports. Mud battles were fought by making small balls of wet clay and placing them on the tips of long willow sticks. By bending and swinging the long sticks, the balls of mud would fly through the air and splatter on the enemy.

The grandfathers of the tribe often took it upon themselves to make so-called pop guns for young boys. An ash stem about two inches across and six inches long was pared down smooth, and a hole about the size of the little finger was drilled through with a sharp heated bone or stone. Wads of soft green bark, cut from red willow and chewed into a soft mass, were placed into one end of the bored hole and wedged in with a cherry stem ramrod. Turning the end around, another wad was rammed into the opposite hole about half way. After the two ends were wadded, the rod was rammed down with a quick stroke. A loud bang resulted, and boys could play they were fighting enemy tribes.

From childhood, boys and girls learned all the songs that go with the various ceremonial dances. On certain occasions they would be allowed to take actual part in the tribal dances. When this rare privilege was granted, they had their faces painted and their hair groomed with animal fat. When boys grew old enough to become warriors because of deeds of courage and bravery, they could dance and take part in all ceremonies.

In the evenings, however, boys and girls would listen

around the campfires and in the family lodges to the telling of legends and great deeds by the old warriors.

Today, most Indian boys and girls live on reservations and go to school. As there are many areas where Indian and white families live side by side, some Indian boys and girls attend public country or town schools near their homes. Many children go to Government, or church boarding schools on the reservations, while others are taken away from the reservations and enrolled in Federal non-reservation schools such as those at Pierre and Flandreau in South Dakota, and Pipestone, Minnesota.

Indian children love to draw—especially horses. They are taught in school to weave cloth, make dishes from clay, and cook on electric stoves, as well as to do arithmetic and write good English.

Although Indian boys have adopted football, basketball, and baseball, they still love the open prairie. Instead of using bows and arrows, today they hunt with modern rifles or shotguns for birds, snakes, and rabbits. Large pony herds are a thing of the past with the Sioux, but Indian boys on the reservation are still seen riding horses bareback. Girls still do much of the work at home, but they dress prettily in modern styles.

SONGS AND STORIES

The songs and stories of the Sioux are very old. They have been handed down by word of mouth for generations.

Most of the songs were sung at dances. Indians have always liked to sing, and many knew the words and tom-tom beats to a hundred songs. The most popular of the present-day Sioux dances is the Rabbit Dance in which many songs are sung. The people sing while they dance, and the meter and rhythm is beaten out on the tom-toms. There is a love song heard today at pow-wows in the Sisseton country that when translated, reads:

> When I leave you, I'll be thinking of you
> And while I'm gone, I'll have my mind toward you.

Another song of the Rabbit Dance is:

Cousin, here we both dance
   (Cepanci he-tu-we keci waci so)
Cousin, tell him I wish to talk to him
   (Cepanci okey-ake ye keci wowagla kin kte)
Cousin, tell him he is the one I like
   (Cepanci okey-ake ye he wasta wilake)
In time he can see me
   (To-kesa wan-mayan ke kta) (Iya-ha-ha-yo)

Couples in the Rabbit Dance form a circle, with each pair facing the backs of the couple in front. The steps are short and at a certain beat of the tom-tom each couple whirls around in a small circle and then continues forward.

Of the old dances, the Sun Dance was the most famous. It was prohibited by the Federal Government in 1881 because of the torture it caused, but occasionally simple parts of it are held on the reservations on special occasions. In the Sun Dance, buckskin strips from a center pole were fastened to the skin of men's chests and the warriors danced for hours until the flesh was torn away. The Horse Dance, which was performed on horses, and the Fox Dance were discontinued many years ago.

During the Messiah War of 1890 the Ghost Dance was introduced. The dancers wore sacred shirts which they believed would keep out bullets. One of the Ghost dance songs, sung by the people as they moved in a large circle, was as follows:

> Mother, oh come back
> *(Ina hekuya)*
> Mother, oh come back
> *(Ina hekuya)*
> Little brother calls as he seeks thee, weeping
> *(Misunkala ceya-ya-omani)*
> Little brother calls as he seeks thee, weeping
> *(Misunkala ceya-ya-omani)*
> Mother, oh come back
> *(Ina hekuya)*
> Mother, oh, come back
> *(Ina hekuya)*
> Says the Father
> *(Ate heya-lo)*
> Says the Father
> *(Ate heya-lo)*

Nowadays many of the younger Indians dance the same as white people—some are real jitterbugs. But on the reservations the native Owl Dance, Legion Dance, Rabbit Dance, and Grass Dance are still seen at pow-wows.

It is real enjoyment to hear an old Indian tell a legend of his tribe. He unravels the story so quietly and so

The native dances are still seen at powwows.

easily that he seems to be thinking in the clouds. Then he will come to a joke or a prank, and his eyes seem to laugh. Sometimes if the story is exciting, or has a battle in it, the old man will make signs with his hands. It makes the listener feel as if he were a part of the story.

Many of the legends have been told and heard many times. Grandfathers told the stories to their grandsons, and when the grandsons became old men they told them to their children's children. Some legends are very, very old, while others are stories of things that have happened since the white men came.

Today sometimes there are several stories almost alike because in different tribes the storytellers have changed something or added something. The old men of the Sioux tribes still love to tell their legends. So that all young people can enjoy these stories, most of the best ones are related in this book.

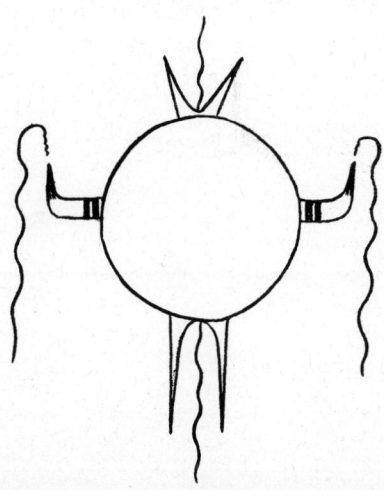

2. Traditional Lore

HOW THE SIOUX NATION WAS BORN

THE Sioux people do not claim to be related to any other people in the whole world. They do not say, as we do, that their ancestors were German or English or Norwegian Vikings. According to their oldest legends, the Sioux tell of very unusual ancestors.

Many, many winters ago when the world was young, a great flood visited the western plains. Many tribes came to the "hills of the prairies" to get away from the rising waters. These hills are near the present towns of Pipestone, Minnesota, and Flandreau, South Dakota. In the lands of the rising and setting suns, nations were destroyed from the earth. The water continued to rise on the hills until it covered all the people. Their flesh and blood was turned into red pipestone, say the wise old grandfathers.

While the tribes were drowning, a big, bald eagle flew down so that a beautiful maiden could catch hold of its feet. The eagle carried her away to the top of a great tree on a high cliff above the water.

Up on this cliff, when the water went down again, the girl had twins and their father was the war eagle!

They began a new tribe that was strong and brave. It was in this manner that a great nation was born. The pipestone which was the flesh of their ancestors is smoked as a symbol of peace. The eagle's feather is worn on the heads of Sioux braves. The land of the pipestone still belongs to all tribes alike.

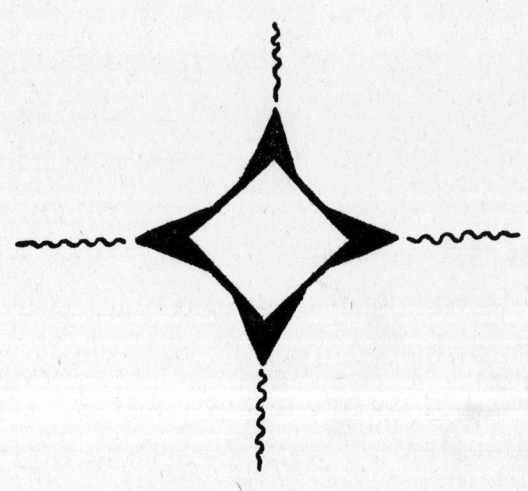

THE BIRTH OF A TRIBE

Here is another story told at campfires about how the Sioux Nation was born.

At the beginning of time, a race of people lived under the waters of a great sea far to the east. They were brave and strong and in a happy land. No one grew old or weak.

One day one of them, more adventurous than the rest, climbed out onto the bank which formed the shore line, and found himself in the bright sunshine of a new land. The grass was soft and green, a color which he had never before seen. The shade of the trees furnished delightful coolness, and he danced and sang.

When at last he was tired and wanted to return, he could not find the sea again. After much walking he found the sea, but there was a great wall. He could not return, so he called to his friends under the sea.

At last one of them, a friendly maiden, heard his call. With great effort, she climbed over the wall to help him. She also found it was impossible to return. At last, driven by hunger, they were forced to hunt for food. They met hardships of many kinds; the hills and thickets made travel hard for their bare feet. Strange animals frightened them; food was hard to find.

Finally, they reached the shore of a great river. There they paused to rest and decided to remain. The country of the great Father of Waters—the Mississippi River—was kind to them. In their new home they grew strong and sure of themselves, and were the ancestors of a great tribe of brave warriors—the Sioux.

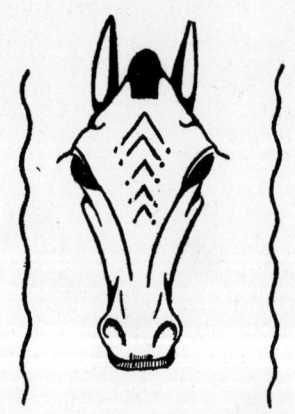

THE GIFT OF THE PEACE PIPE

IN the early days of Indian life, old legends tell that the seven campfires of the Sioux tribes burned in the Land of the Rising Sun.

One day two young men were hunting wild game for their village. There were not many large animals in the region and the people were hungry. While wading through snowdrifts among the trees, they were startled to see a beautiful woman standing before them. She was dressed in pretty robes, and in her hand she held a small bundle. The two young men could not think of anything to say, so they just stood and looked at the woman.

"Do not fear," said the woman. "I bring you peace and happiness. Now tell me, why are you so far from your village?"

Her grace and beauty so fired the older brave with

love that he could not speak. Finally the younger man spoke.

"Our village is in need of more food," he said. "We are hunting."

"Here," she said, "take this bundle back to your people. Tell the Chiefs of the seven campfires to meet in the council lodge and wait for me."

The two men still could think of nothing to say. The older brave, blinded by love for the beautiful woman, reached out to touch her. As he did so, she touched him lightly on the head and he fell to the ground. Then, as suddenly as she had appeared, she disappeared.

The older brave was ashamed and followed the younger man back to the village. The next day the seven Chiefs put on their best feathers and robes and sat in a circle, all looking down at the bundle which had not been opened.

A sudden blow of wind passed. When it had gone the Chiefs saw before them a beautiful woman dressed in pretty robes. None of them could find words in their mouths. So she spoke to them:

"I bring you a message of peace. Your people are great hunters and brave warriors. When the sun rises again, pack your belongings and travel toward the setting sun. There a great land awaits you. You will find beyond the Father of Waters new animals and other tribes of people. In this bundle is a pipe to bring you peace with all people."

The woman took out a pipe made from bone and decorated with bird feathers. Then she left the lodge and disappeared.

Soon the tribes moved westward. They came to the Mississippi River which was called the Father of Waters, and then to the Missouri River and the Black Hills. They saw for the first time the animals we call horses, and there were great herds of buffalo.

To make peace with other tribes, the Sioux chieftains brought out their peace pipe. The pipe was usually handed to the Chief of the enemy tribe first and then it was smoked by all the leaders of both tribes. Later, when the white men came to the Sioux country, the Indians brought out their pipe of peace to smoke.

A great amount of soft red stone was found for making pipes and every year all the Sioux tribes would send some of their people to the pipestone quarries to smoke the pipe of peace with other tribes. This place came to be known as Pipestone, the name which it carries to this day as a town and Indian school in Minnesota.

HOW THE TWO KETTLE BAND WAS NAMED

SNOWSTORMS often come suddenly and without warning. On such a day some years ago a party of Sioux hunters and their families became snowbound far from their village. The wind blew so hard and the snow was so thick that the Indians could not see to travel. Soon the piles of snow were too deep to walk through.

A camp was made, but before long they were out of food. Finally the storm ended. Now they could start home. As the snow melted it made big rivers out of little ones, and small rivers where before there had been none. The going was slow, and everyone became very hungry.

When some of the people became so weary and starved that they could not go on, a scout came running to tell them he had found a deserted village. The people hurried on to see if anything to eat had been thrown away.

How the Two Kettle Band Was Named

One brave walked into a grove of small trees and bushes. There he found a bundle, tied with strips of rawhide. He quickly opened it. In it was enough dried meat to fill two kettles.

He called out that he had found meat for two kettles. Everyone was happy again, and a fire was built. After they had eaten they were strong enough to continue the journey and soon returned to their village.

When the Chief of the tribe heard them tell of their trip, he called them the Two Kettle Band. To this day relatives of these people live on the Rosebud Indian Reservation. They are known as the Two Kettle Band.

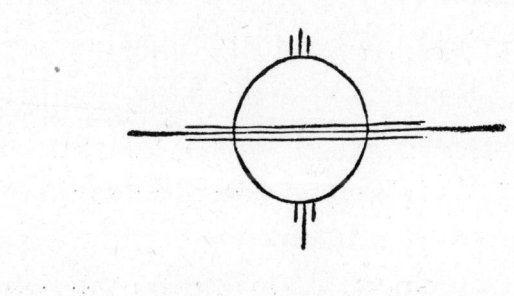

BURNT HIP

THERE was once a man named Burnt Hip who had bad thoughts in his heart. He had four sons who, together with their father, were responsible for several deaths in the Rosebud country. They quarreled with everyone and tried to make all people afraid of them.

One day Burnt Hip heard of a man who looked like him. For the simple reason that this man did resemble him, Burnt Hip decided to kill the man.

It so happened that someone overheard Burnt Hip talking about his evil plans, so he hurried along the creek to warn High Elk, the man who looked like the bad Indian.

High Elk lived with his sister, White Feather. When he learned of Burnt Hip's evil plans, he told his sister to take his tomahawk and have it ready in case Burnt Hip should get the better of him. Soon afterward Burnt

Hip arrived. He came forward and the battle was on.

After they had fought for some time, High Elk felt himself weakening. He called to his sister to help him. Each time that Burnt Hip was on top, High Elk would call to his sister to strike the enemy. But Burnt Hip, being a clever Indian, soon spoiled that. When High Elk was on top, Burnt Hip too would call to her to strike. White Feather was very puzzled, for they were so much alike that she did not know her brother from the enemy.

Then High Elk noticed the deep scar on the hip of his foe. Waiting until Burnt Hip was again nearest to White Feather, he called to her to hit the one with a scar on his hip. She hit him with a mighty blow and Burnt Hip fell over dead.

Knowing that the four sons of Burnt Hip were sure to come, High Elk and White Feather buried the body under their campfire. Then High Elk said, "When they arrive, we will get under one blanket and sit very close together and as Burnt Hip and I look so much alike, they will think that I am Burnt Hip."

When the four sons came and looked inside the teepee, they saw the man they thought was their father sitting with this woman. They went away happy, thinking that their father had won the fight and had taken a new wife. As soon as they were gone, High Elk and his sister packed up their belongings and moved far away.

A band of Sioux still bears the name of Burnt Hip.

The Burnt Hip Band is not the same as the Sioux tribe known as the Brules (brūlēēs), which means Burnt Thighs or Burned Backs. Once a tribe of Sioux warriors made a raid against the Pawnees in what is now Nebraska. Pawnee scouts, however, saw the raiding party coming. The Pawnees quietly set fire to the prairie around the Sioux warriors and caught the raiders in a trap of flames. Most of the Sioux escaped but were severely burned. When they returned to the Sioux country, tribesmen jokingly called them *Sicangu,* which means "burned thighs." The word was later translated by French traders as *brule* which is the French word for burned.

THE OWL'S WARNING

SWAN, a young Sioux boy, liked to study tracks, signals, and the other things a warrior must know in scouting the enemy. He wanted to grow up to be a famous scout in his tribe.

One winter when the village supplies were very low, the chief called Swan to his lodge. The Chief said he did not wish to send the braves on a distant hunting trip for fear the enemy might attack the camp while the warriors were away. So he asked Swan to scout the location of the enemy. He was told to bring back news of their strength, both in horses and warriors.

Swan started early in the morning and all day long he traveled without a stop for food. He watched every sign—in the air, on the ground, and in the bushes and trees. At nightfall he placed his small teepee under a large tree near a fine spring of water and decided to eat and rest for a time, until the moon should give him some light to see his way. He killed a bird and cooked it over a campfire in the teepee.

Swan was very tired, but he knew he must prepare his arrows, for he felt that he was in enemy country. Sitting by his fire, Swan carefully ground the edges of an arrow between two flat stones to make the point sharper. He was so intent upon his work that when an owl in a tree over his tent softly called "Who-oo, who-oo," it seemed so close that he was startled and dropped his arrow.

Swan realized the noise had been made by an owl. As he bent over to pick up the arrow again, his eyes rested on the surface of a bowl of water he had placed near his fire when he was getting his evening meal. To his great surprise, Swan saw, reflected in the water, the face of an enemy looking down at him through the smoke hole in the top of his teepee. Showing no sign of having seen the enemy face, Swan continued to sharpen his arrows, placing them within easy reach. He tested his bow also. Then, with a quick twist of the wrist, he shot an arrow straight up through the face looking down at him. The enemy scout fell over dead.

Swan took the enemy's scalp and set out at once to

Swan saw the face of an enemy looking down.

find the camp. He discovered it not very far away. After learning the number of warriors, the size of the village, and all the things which his people would want to know, he ran fast, careful to leave no trace of his visit.

When he arrived in his home village and told his story, the wise old man said: "Ha, the owl is a very wise bird. It brings a warning that danger is near or that danger is approaching."

After that the scouts and many of the others in the Sioux Nation learned to hoot like an owl as a signal of danger.

THE SNAIL AND THE BEAVER

ONCE upon a time a snail basked in the warm sunshine, passing a quiet life on the banks of a river. A flood came, washing against the shore and hurrying the water of the usually slow stream. The snail was swept into the current and carried to a greater river, where the waves left him again upon the shore.

The heat of a summer sun beat upon him and he grew big. He saw many brave warriors who came to the river, and he tried to become strong like them. His ambition was so great that his nature changed and he became a man.

In his new life he tried to find the land where he had first lived as a snail. The way was long and he became hungry and tired. Then the Mighty Spirit appeared, gave him a bow and arrow, taught him how to kill and to cook game, and showed him how to cover himself with skins. Then he continued his journey and finally found the land where he had once lived.

He approached the river which had once made music in his ear. He sunned himself on the same sand where long ago he had been only a snail. Suddenly he was met by a beaver who claimed the land as his own. A battle began and lasted until the daughter of the beaver appeared. She made peace between them.

Soon after she and the man who had been a snail were married. From this union grew a tribe that has ever since refused to shoot a beaver.

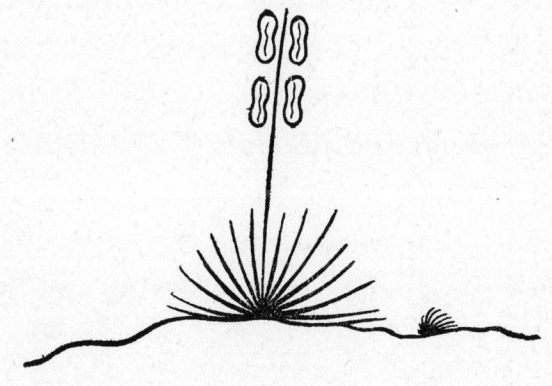

HOW THE RAINBOW CAME TO BE

ONE bright summer day when all the flowers were out, nodding their heads in the breeze and proudly showing their many beautiful colors, the Mighty Spirit overheard one of the older flowers saying to another:

"I wonder where we will go when winter comes and we all must die? It doesn't seem fair. We do our share to make the earth a beautiful place to live in. Should we not also go to a happy hunting ground of our own?"

The Mighty Spirit thought about this and decided that they should not die when winter came. So now after a refreshing shower, we may look up in the sky and see all the pretty, colored flowers of the past year making a beautiful rainbow across the heavens.

In the sky are all the flowers.

WHY THE BABY DEER WEARS SPOTS

YEARS ago when the spirits still roamed the earth, one of them happened to be sitting by a fire recounting the deeds he had done for the many creatures he knew.

"I have helped almost every creature," he said. "I have made feathers for the birds so they may flock together and flee from their enemies; I gave the porcupine his quills, the buffalo his horns, the wolf his strong teeth, the deer and rabbit their speed. In fact, nearly every creature has received from me some form of defense to use whenever he is in need."

The Spirit soon realized his error, however, when a mother deer sped to his side, closely followed by her fawn, or baby deer.

"Oh, Spirit," she said, "you gave to me my speed, and to others you have given some means of protection, but how is such a young one to keep away from enemies?"

"I will take care of that," replied the Spirit. "I shall make him so hard to see that he will be safe while hiding, and no animal shall ever find him by his smell."

So taking his brush and paints he carefully painted spots upon the fawn's body until he blended with the shadows in the grass and brush.

From then on the mother found that she could eat while the fawn hid, and although the spots disappear when the fawn is full grown, he no longer needs them, for the gift of speed protects him.

HOW DUCKS GOT THEIR COLORS

A YOUNG warrior, who from childhood had been very fond of bright colors, walked far from camp. He loved the beautiful colors of Indian summer. Now and then he would stop and take from his pouch some clay and oil to paint the colors he saw. As the shadows grew long, he knew that it would soon be time for the night fire, so he made his way to a nearby lake where he built a small lodge.

As he sat looking at the red sun which was about to go down under the colored sky, he heard the talk of waterfowl coming toward him. He saw large and small ducks, gray geese, and loons diving and playing. They were all his friends and he was glad to see them. He cupped his hands about his mouth and called to them. They were startled at first, but when they recognized him they paddled to shore.

The young man invited them all to his lodge. There they visited and took turns telling what they had done that day. When the young warrior told them that he had been studying and mixing colors, a gray duck became interested.

"You are our friend," said the duck. "Would you be so kind as to paint us with some of your beautiful colors?"

"I will," the warrior answered. "Now choose your colors."

The large gray duck decided that he wished a pretty green head with a white stripe around his neck, a brown breast, and yellow legs. When he was painted, the duck flapped his wings. Ducks with these colors are now called mallard ducks.

"I hope you will not paint my mate with the same colors I have," he said.

So she was painted mostly brown.

Then the teal had himself and his family painted as he desired. By this time the paints were almost gone, so there were no bright colors left for the goose and the loon.

WHY THE LEAVES FALL

MANY moons ago when the world was still very young, the plant and animal life was enjoying the beautiful summer weather. But as the days went by, autumn set in, and the weather became colder with each passing day.

The grass and flower folk were in a sad condition, for they had no protection from the sharp cold. Just when it seemed that there was no hope for living, He who looks after the things of His creation came to their aid. He said that the leaves of the trees should fall to the ground, spreading a soft, warm blanket over the tender roots of the grass and flowers. To repay the trees for the loss of their leaves, He allowed them one last bright array of beauty.

That is why, each year, during Indian summer the trees take on their pretty farewell colors of red, gold, and brown. After this final display they turn to their appointed task—covering the earth with a thick rug of warmth against the chill of winter.

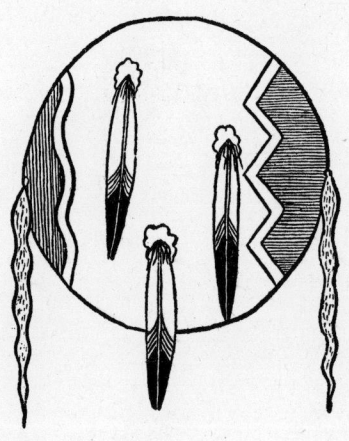

The trees take on their farewell colors.

3. Campfire Tales

THE STORY OF A HARD WINTER

Once there lived in a teepee of buffalo robes four brothers and a sister. They had grown up happily together near the lake which was their home.

After a summer during which all four brothers had been hurt in raids among enemy tribes, the hard winter found them ill and unable to hunt.

Only the sister was well. The sick brothers were badly in need of food so that they could become strong again. When the cold, hard winter came, all the sister could do was to hunt for berries that had not been picked in the fall—rose berries, gooseberries, and sage. To keep her brothers alive, she cooked the berries that could be found above the drifted snow.

While picking berries one day, the sister saw a buffalo running in her direction. A strange Indian on horseback was chasing the buffalo. The man drew back his bow, and with one arrow he shot the buffalo in the heart. The buffalo stumbled and fell. It dropped to the ground close to the place where the sister was standing.

Without any words, the stranger skinned the buffalo. He cut out the meat and after placing it in the skin, he sewed up the edges in the form of a big bag. Then he threw it over his shoulder. Without as much as a single word to the girl, he rode away.

The sister cried as she thought how her four brothers needed the meat. A few small bits of meat were left, and she picked them up. Then she swiftly carried the pieces home to be mixed with berries for soup.

The brothers recognized the taste of meat. They demanded to know where the meat had come from. She told them of the strange man, saying, "I met a man who killed a buffalo, but although I stood beside him, he offered me none."

The brothers became very angry. They said that if they ever became well again they would find the man who refused to help their sister.

A few days later, while the girl was gathering up left-over berries, the stranger killed another buffalo. She stood even closer this time, watching him pack the meat into the hide bag, but again he failed to speak.

A third time it happened. This time after the stranger sewed the skin into a bag, he turned to the sister, saying: "Take this home to your four sick brothers."

"It is too heavy for me to carry," she said.

"If you will put the bag over your shoulder and without looking back, walk straight home, the burden will be light," he answered.

She picked up the huge skin full of meat. She could carry it easily. As the sister walked away she kept thinking about the stranger who knew that her brothers were ill and who could make her big burden so light. She was so curious to see if he was still watching her that she glanced back! Suddenly the burden bore her down on her knees.

The stranger rode his pony up to her and said: "You must never disobey my words." Then he told her to shoulder the load again and not to look back. This time she obeyed.

When her four brothers saw the meat, they crawled across the dirt floor to it. She had a hard time keeping the hungry men from eating it before it was cooked.

Soon the brothers were strong again. When spring came they were ready to hunt.

The four brothers called their sister to them one evening. The oldest one said, "Sister, we think you are a fine woman. We would like you to marry the man who saved us from starving—to pay him back for helping us. You should go to him. He may need a wife."

The sister said she would do as they wished. She packed her belongings and walked all day. In the evening, while walking through a grove of trees, she saw a teepee. She entered it. The stranger was sitting there, making arrows. She shyly told him that she was sent by her brothers whose lives he had saved. For that deed she was ready to become his wife.

The stranger replied that his parents had told him never to marry as long as he lived. He gave her presents of moccasins and arrows, and told her to return to her four brothers. When she was ready to start home it was late in the evening. She was afraid. There were wolves howling and other noises in the woods. She bravely walked all night, arriving home the next day. When she told her brothers of her trip, they again became angry at the man because he had refused to marry their pretty sister.

Winter came again. The four brothers decided they would frighten the stranger out of the country for not marrying their sister. One evening they put on their war paint and went to his camp. They surrounded the wigwam, making sounds of owls, bears, coyotes, wolves, and bobcats—the warning given by enemies before a raid is made.

When the stranger heard the sounds, he ran quickly out of the teepee into the forest.

The four brothers and their sister moved into the hunter's deserted teepee which was large and comfortable. They believed its owner had left forever.

While the sister was picking up wood a few days later, she saw the man they had frightened. He was hiding in a hollow tree for shelter. He was shivering from the cold. The girl cried with sadness. She told him how sorry she was. He then asked for his moccasins, buckskin hunting suit, snowshoes, and bow and arrows, telling her that everything else in the teepee she could keep.

When she brought him his belongings that he asked for, he told her he was a *Wakan,* one who had great and unusual powers—a medicine man.

He said to her that in a nearby teepee there was a stuffed white buffalo which had bags of medicine tied to each horn. In the pouch on the right horn a charm was kept to be used for hunting buffaloes. He said that if she would take out some of the mystic medicine and make a fire out of it in front of the buffalo, out of the smoke would come a real live buffalo!

The stranger warned her that the first buffalo coming out of the smoke must be shot. If it was not shot, an entire herd of buffalo would come out of the smoke.

After the stranger left, she went to tell her brothers who had returned from a hunting trip. They did not believe in the *Wakan's* power to create buffaloes. So they made a fire of the medicine in the bag. White smoke filled the teepee. Then, to their surprise, out of the smoke came a large, live buffalo. The four brothers raised their bows and let fly their arrows. The smoke cleared away and they had a feast. After that whenever they became hungry more buffaloes were shot in the way the *Wakan* had said.

Another spring came and the four brothers decided to go on a trip into the country of the enemy. They were to be gone many days on their raids. The sister stayed at home alone. Before the brothers left, they told their sister not to listen to anyone who talked to her and never to tell a man the secret of the white buffalo.

They had been gone a full moon when, one day, Unktomee came to the teepee. Unktomee was a short man with a hump on his back. He was known to do strange and evil things. Unktomee looked around the teepee and saw the mounted white buffalo. It caused him to wonder. He believed that the buffalo had strange powers.

He also noticed that in the teepee there were five dishes. Knowing that it was the custom for each person to have a dish of his own, Unktomee knew that there must be four brothers away.

"I met your four brothers," he said to the woman, making a guess that the dishes belonged to brothers.

The sister was very anxious to hear about them; so she broke her vow not to talk. She asked about her brothers.

"They told me to go to their lodge to hunt buffalo. They said you would tell me how," he said.

The sister believed his story. She told him the secret.

Unktomee started a fire with the medicine. Then he stood by the flap of the teepee with his arrow ready to shoot. But instead of killing the first buffalo that came out of the smoke, Unktomee watched it go outside!

Out of the smoke came more buffaloes—ten, fifteen, twenty, thirty, forty. A great herd ran by. Unktomee was not able to stop them. His eyes grew big like one who has not long to live.

The buffaloes started running in a circle. There was no escape for Unktomee. The buffaloes stamped him under their hoofs!

The girl stood in the doorway of the teepee crying. While she was standing there, a buffalo that walked on its back legs understood her and came near. In animal language he told her to get on the back of the largest and strongest buffalo in the herd. She did as he said.

The herd headed west. It had been gone about two days when the brothers returned from the war party. Their sister was gone. Unktomee was trampled to death. The brothers knew what had come about.

The eldest brother said he would follow the tracks of the buffaloes. Gathering up all his arrows and those of his brothers, he started out. Soon he saw the herd in the distance. He saw how one buffalo walked on its rear legs. It was lagging behind. The brother came up to the two-legged buffalo.

"What has happened, and where is my sister?" the brother asked.

"She is riding the strongest buffalo in the herd," the animal said. "They always wait for me to catch up. If you would kill me and wear my skin, you could go into the herd and talk to your sister."

The brother took the buffalo's advice and shot him. He put on the hide and walked into the herd. He came near the buffalo carrying his sister:

"Sister, I am here. I have come to take you back. You must ride behind me until the rest get ahead of us. Then we will turn around toward our home," he said.

A buffalo heard the brother talking. The buffalo was very angry. He called the herd to follow him. The sister fell off and ran to her brother.

The buffaloes began running in a circle. They were going to stamp down the girl and her brother who wore the buffalo skin. The brother dropped off the skin, and told his sister to keep handing him arrows. He killed the leader of the herd and the next few stumbled over the body, breaking their necks. He shot more buffalo and many others fell over the dead ones. The herd became afraid and ran away, leaving the sister and brother alone.

So the brother took his sister home and they all lived happily once more.

IKTOMI SEEKS A BRIDE

MANY years ago the daughter of a chief was to marry a brave young warrior who was known for his skill as a hunter with bow and arrow.

The chief sent word to the young brave that he first must show his skill to prove that he was worthy of her.

When the young warrior received the word he at once set about to prepare himself for whatever task the chief might have him do. For hours at a time he shot arrows at a pine cone set at the foot of a tree many paces away. Then he sharpened his eye for moving targets by throwing a stone high into a cottonwood tree and shooting arrows through the leaves as they fell to the ground.

"The chief's daughter is the most beautiful in all the tribes and I will be a lucky man if I can win her," thought the young warrior as he walked through the woods in the direction of the chief's camp.

He was nearing the camp when a stranger appeared. The two greeted each other and then sat down to talk.

"I have been invited by the chief to show my skill with bow and arrow," said the young warrior, "and if I can please him I will be given the hand of his daughter in marriage. Would you not like to be in my place?"

"I will not believe you are good enough to win the chief's daughter until you show me your skill," said the stranger. "Shoot an arrow into the highest branch of that tree," he said as he pointed to a tall pine whose top seemed to reach nearly to the sky.

The young warrior at once placed an arrow on his bowstring and let it go. Up and up it went to the highest branch where its point struck firmly in the wood.

"Now let me see you climb the tree and get the arrow," said the stranger.

The young warrior quickly climbed the tree and was nearly back to the ground when the stranger pulled a buffalo-hide rope from under his blanket and tied him fast to the trunk.

"Now," laughed the stranger, "you will stay here and I will go to the chief's camp and claim his daughter. I am Iktomi."

"You say you are Iktomi, hated by all good Indians?"

"I see your heart is bad toward me," replied Iktomi, "but it will be worse after I have taken the chief's daughter for my bride. I will be far away by the time you get loose and tell the chief what happened."

Iktomi laughed—an ugly, wicked laugh. Taking the young warrior's bow and arrows, he made his way toward the camp of the chief.

"Your good message came to me," said Iktomi to the chief, "and I am ready to prove that I am good enough to take your daughter for my wife. I am brave and strong."

The chief greeted him cordially and took him to his wigwam. There Iktomi was fed the choicest cuts of buffalo and deer meat and given cool sweet water from a nearby spring. In the meantime the chief sent word to his people that the young man who was so skillful with bow and arrow had arrived. The tribesmen and their wives and children quickly gathered around the chief's teepee.

The first task ordered by the chief was to shoot a rabbit as it was chased past the teepee. Iktomi placed an arrow on his bowstring. As the rabbit bounded past, he let the shaft fly. The arrow went wide of the rabbit and buried its tip in the ground.

"That was not a fair test," complained Iktomi. "My blanket blew against my arm as I shot."

But by this time the young warrior had freed himself from the buffalo-hide rope that held him to the tree and came running into camp. There he told of the trick Iktomi had played on him. The chief was very angry and ordered Iktomi tied and severely beaten, after which he was driven from camp.

Then the young warrior was given his chance to prove his skill. The rabbit was again chased past the teepee. Straight to the mark flew the arrow and the rabbit was fastened to the ground. The chief was pleased with the handsome young warrior and led forth his daughter.

"She is yours," said the chief, "and from now on you are one of my people."

The young warrior could hardly believe his eyes, for the daughter was the most beautiful maiden he had ever seen.

"I am indeed a lucky man," said the warrior, "and all my life I will do my best to make her happy."

That night a great feast was held to celebrate the marriage of the chief's daughter and the brave young warrior.

BEAVER IMAGE

THERE lived among a roaming band of Sioux a young brave and his beautiful wife. The woman came from the family of a great warrior and she was loved for her kindness and her desire to help people.

One day while the braves were out hunting buffalo and the women were busy gathering wild fruits for winter use, the young wife went to the spring to get water for the day.

She sat down to admire the beauties of nature and stayed longer than she thought.

Rising, she took her rawhide bucket and stooped to fill the bucket. Suddenly from beneath the bank under her feet, a beaver jumped into the water. The woman dropped her bucket and made piercing screams of fright as she ran toward the village.

Everyone in the village was aroused and rushed

quickly to the aid of the young wife. She told of her experience with the beaver. This happening was looked upon as an evil omen by the women of the tribe.

Upon hearing this evil omen, the young wife became ill. One day soon a son was born and she became very happy in the care of the child.

When the baby was a month old, he began to have spells of crying all night. The mother, having tried every means of quieting the child, finally called the Medicine Man.

He took the baby and gave the child a drink from a buffalo-horn spoon. Then he filled his hands with water and sprinkled the boy's body. The child immediately fell asleep. The Medicine Man then told the mother that he feared the child would have the ways of a beaver. He bestowed the title of Beaver Image on the boy. Ever afterwards the mother gave her baby the same treatment whenever he cried at night.

When the boy was two winters old the mother found that he was never satisfied unless he could play in water. In spite of all the help of the women of the tribe, the child was unable to talk. Instead he made sounds like those of a beaver. The boy continued to behave in this manner, staying in the water most of the time. His parents had to force him to leave the water and come home for food and sleep. He liked to feed on fish and chew on trees. If some Indian stopped and looked at him, he would strike and bite like a beaver. During the night he would gather large piles of sticks and place them in a row along the river banks, as if preparing to build a beaver dam.

Thus he lived for many winters along the river, becoming known to all the Sioux as Beaver Image.

After many years Beaver Image acquired a fierce look, his skin turned black from exposure and hardships, and his body was covered with coarse hair. On his head his hair grew long and fell below his shoulders in a tangled mass. His long nails and his toes were said to be as dangerous as the claws of a wild animal.

Such was the creature that the Sioux learned to fear. When children failed to obey their parents, they were told the story of Beaver Image.

FLEETFOOT

MANY years ago a little fawn by the name of Fleetfoot lived in the big woods with his father and mother.

Fleetfoot, so named because he was such a fleet and fast runner, ate the moss, leaves, and berries that Nature provided.

Fleetfoot had only one enemy. The enemy was Wild Bird, an Indian who lived in a teepee nearby and often painted his face and arms. To Wild Bird's wife went the task of putting up the teepee and planting the corn.

She also made baskets of rushes and put colors on moccasins.

One day food was needed; so Wild Bird told his wife he was going hunting to kill a deer. He went to the middle of the forest. At the same time Fleetfoot's mother said, "Go at once and get some berries and moss. Hurry, for our food is gone."

"All right," sang out Fleetfoot as he sped away.

He was soon a great distance from home when suddenly a strange sound caught his ears. He stopped short and listened, but the sound stopped also. So he ran on and on until whom should he see but Wild Bird with his bow and arrows. He turned and again fled, but this time in a different direction until finally he had lost his enemy.

"Now I'll go home," thought Fleetfoot. But alas! Where was home? He was lost, for every direction seemed the way home to him.

It was lucky for Fleetfoot that he was lost because Wild Bird came upon two deer and killed them. They were Fleetfoot's mother and father.

Fleetfoot grew to a great size with large antlers, and he lived to rule a great band of deer in the Black Hills.

PUTTING THE BEE ON BRUIN

Long before white people came to America, wild creatures roamed about the country living off the land, never harming each other as they do today.

Among the animals, snakes, birds, and bugs, the bee was considered the best worker. The bee visited the flowers and made honey to use during the winter.

The bear was the most lazy. Never did the huge, shaggy creature leave his den until he could no longer stand the hunger he felt. Then he would go out and steal from the winter pouches of other creatures.

One day, while the bear was searching for something to eat, he came upon a hollow tree. In it lived a great swarm of bees. Bruin the bear saw the many tiny winged creatures coming to and going from the tree. He was so curious that he put his paw into the hole, right into the bees' honey. Everything the bear touched stuck to his paw, so he started to lick off the sticky honey. It was good to eat! He ate and ate the sweet honey until he was full.

Day after day the bear came to the hollow tree to steal honey. Then one day, the queen bee called to the Mighty Spirit, asking that the bear be taken away, or that they be given some way to defend their honey. The Mighty Spirit gave them sharp stingers as weapons.

One day soon Bruin became hungry and again visited the hollow tree. His mouth watered at the thought of the sweet honey waiting there. He put his big paw into the hollow tree, but instead of getting covered with honey, it was covered with bees. Some of them also jumped on his nose, some in his ears, some dug into his hide.

The huge animal rolled and roared. His eyes, lips, and tongue began to swell, and his body was full of stingers. He ran away as fast as he could.

From that day the laboring bees have seldom been troubled by a bear or other animals.

THE SUN GAZER

ONCE there was a boy who early in life had a deep love for the sun. For hours each day he would sit and watch the bright sun on its journey across the sky. He would sing many songs in praise of the sunshine. Because of his strange love for the sun, he was named Sun Gazer.

Through his constant looking at the sun he gradually became blind. Yet, guided by the heat of its rays on his face, he followed the sun on its daily course. In the darkness he lost interest in life. Daily he grew weaker, and he was often sad.

One evening after sundown when he did not return from his favorite place on a nearby hill, a party was sent out to search for him. They found him facing the west. The last spark of life had gone from him as the final rays of the sun disappeared.

The searchers buried him on that very spot. The next

morning when they returned to visit the grave, they saw that a tall, graceful flower had sprung from the mound and was gently nodding in the breeze. As they watched, they found that it too followed the sun across the sky.

The flower has come to be known as the sunflower, and at different times of the day, its face is ever turned toward the sun.

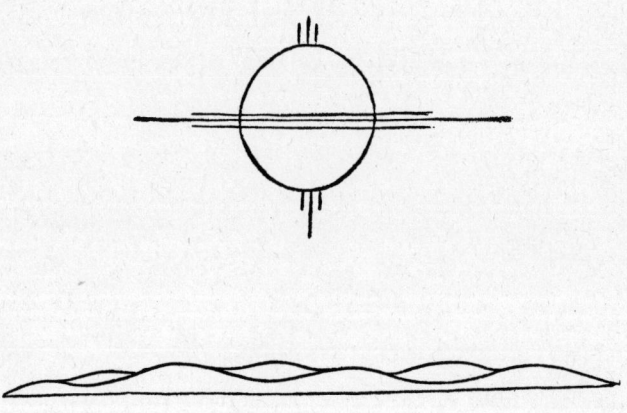

The Sunflower's face is ever turned toward the sun.

THE HUNTER AND THE WOLF

ON a very windy autumn day many years ago a hunter was going about in search of game. As he walked along, he came upon a wolf which had surprised a flock of geese, then had killed a number of them.

The hunter, who was very lazy, was pleased to be able to find some game so easily. He drove the wolf away and began preparing the geese for a big meal for himself.

While the geese were roasting, the man became angry at two nearby trees which were rubbing and squeaking as they moved in the wind. The noise made him very angry and he ordered the trees to stop moving.

When the harsh noise continued, the hunter climbed up into the branches. He placed one leg between the trunks that were rubbing and began to pry them apart, hoping to put an end to the terrifying noise. Just then the wind stopped blowing and the trees came close together. He was held fast between them.

The wolf, watching from a distance, saw what had happened. He went back, ate all the geese, and left only the feet sticking out of the ashes.

Finally the man worked himself loose, only to find that he had gained nothing by letting some one else do his hunting.

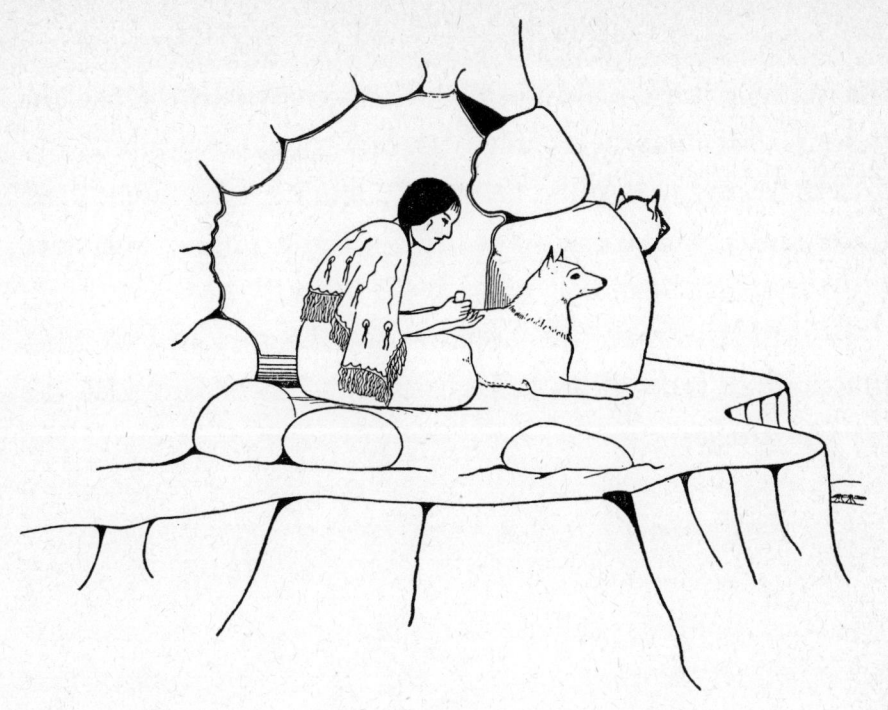

THE WOMAN AND THE WOLVES

WHILE a band of Sioux was hunting in Montana many years ago, one of the men met a young woman whom he wanted to marry. He already had a wife, but he took a new wife anyway. The first wife did not like the new wife so, during the night, the first wife ran away.

She walked for several days. One night she fell asleep on the grassy banks of Cherry Creek. The country along the Cheyenne River, into which Cherry Creek flows, has always been a favorite haunt of wolves. The woman was too tired to be afraid. Suddenly she felt a warm, moist tongue against her cheek. She opened her eyes and saw a she-wolf standing beside her. The wolf led the woman to a cave, and every day the wolf brought fresh meat. Soon the woman learned the language of the wolves who were her friends.

The Indian people heard about the woman who lived with the wolf and some people saw her at a distance. They called her Lives-in-the-Cave.

One day the wolf told Lives-in-a-Cave that her people were nearby. It was time she joined them. Lives-in-a-Cave met the people and went with them to the Rosebud country where she lived the rest of her life.

This story had been told to Indian children of the Cheyenne River Reservation for generations, but the cave was not found until a few years ago. The cave, located in Ziebach County of South Dakota, is full of animal bones. According to the Indians, they are the remains of the animals killed by the she-wolf to feed Lives-in-a-Cave.

THE END OF THE WORLD

An Indian woman is sitting in the moonlight and is sewing with porcupine quills. Near her the fire burns brightly and over the fire a kettle of herbs is boiling. By her side sits a dog that watches her. Occasionally she rises, lays down her work, and stirs the herbs. While she is doing this the dog unravels her work.

This has been going on for thousands of years. As fast as the Indian woman sews, the dog unravels. If she should ever complete her work, the end of the world will come at that instant.

So says the Sioux legend.

4. Legends of Places

THE BLACK HILLS

PAHA SAPA, or the Black Hills, have long been regarded by the Sioux as their holy land. Each year tribes came from great distances to cure illnesses in the warm springs and to hunt wild animals.

A legend of the Sioux, still firmly believed, is that the dark of night turns the rocks into spirits that sing strange songs, awakening the echoes. From holes in rock walls healing waters flow and the people fill their buffalo-horn cups with the clear water and drink it to become pure.

From the great needles of rock that touch the sky the medicine men call the Mighty Spirit.

The great deposits of glistening metals should be used for holy wearing and never sold. The Sioux knew of the gold there long before it was discovered by white men.

The picture paintings on the redstone walls, made long before the coming of the Sioux, are read by holy men as a guide on how to live.

The crystal caves, hidden beneath the ground, have great mystery.

It was on Bear Butte, *Mato Paha,* that the father of Crazy Horse performed the rites of a holy man and was given great powers from the Mighty Spirit, who appeared to him in the form of a bear. Later, in 1876, a great council was held at this butte, where chiefs talked over the giving of the Black Hills to the United States Government.

In days of old, Harney Peak was never climbed by the Sioux because there was a strong belief that it was visited by the Thunder Bird. Legend further adds that whenever the Thunder Bird stopped it caused much lightning and thunder in the Black Hills.

Of all the land losses suffered by the Sioux with the coming of white men, the giving away of the holy Black Hills caused the most sadness.

THE VISION OF BEAR BUTTE

A GREAT ceremony that caused much history took place about 1840 when several bands of Sioux were going to the Black Hills. They were going there to gather wild fruits and cut poles for their teepees.

Camp was made at the foot of a great hill. In the dark of night the father of Crazy Horse walked away from the sleeping village. He climbed to the top of the hill to talk with the Great Spirit. The father of Crazy Horse was a good man. He performed the magic secrets of a holy man.

On this night the father of Crazy Horse raised his hands to the sky and called for the guidance of the Mighty Spirit. He stood all night at the top of the hill, making sad sounds and singing.

The next night the old man called together the leaders of the tribes in the council lodge. A ceremonial pipe was filled and passed to each of the tribe's wise old men.

The father of Crazy Horse told his vision thus: "Last night the Mighty Spirit appeared to me in the form of a bear. He gave to me powers to conquer all earthly beings, including the white men who are coming into our land. I am in my declining years, so I choose to give my great spiritual gift to my son, Crazy Horse, who is young and strong. He will use the gift of the Mighty Spirit to be a great leader of the Sioux."

From this time on the sharply rising hill was known as *Mato Paha,* Bear Butte.

The spiritual power that was given to Crazy Horse as a sacred obligation at Bear Butte is believed by the Sioux to have helped to bring about the complete destruction of the troops of General "Yellow Hair" Custer in a battle called Custer's Last Stand.

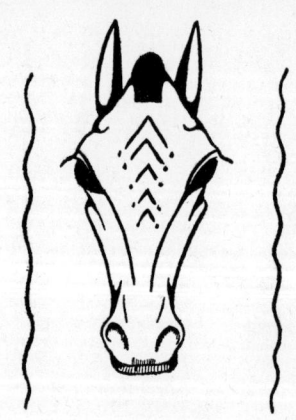

THE GUARDIAN OF THE POOLS

LONG ago there was a great drought even in the Black Hills. The mountain streams no longer sang their way over the rocks. Slowly the streams grew smaller until they were dry, and the grass turned brown. Only the spring in a certain gulch was flowing and water stayed in two pools nearby.

To the pools came all living things. Men, women, and children came to quench their thirst and to forget the hard season. And to the pools also came the beasts—the beavers, deer, bears, and buffaloes, as well as the snakes and burrowing animals.

There was water enough for all, but the animals were not clean and left it dirty. It brought sickness to many of those who had to drink it. No other springs could be found, and the people were very sad.

Then the Mighty Spirit took pity on them and said, "I will send a guardian who will drive away the animals and keep pure the water of the pools."

When morning came the people saw a strange sight. Over the pools stood a woman, tall and stately, her head bowed as she gazed into the precious water.

The stone figure of the woman who guards the pools still stands in the gulch below what is now Sylvan Lake.

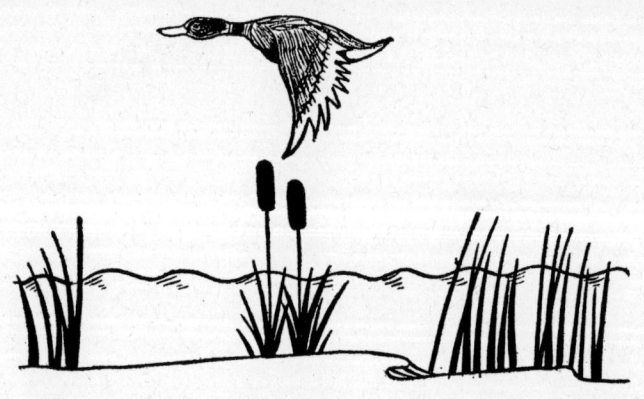

HOW DEVIL'S TOWER CAME TO BE

MANY winters ago in the land of *Paha Sapa,* Black Hills, there lived two small boys.

One day when no one was watching them, the two boys decided to go on a hunting trip of their own. They wanted to find out what the rest of the world was like. All day they walked, looking at the country and eating much wild fruit along the way. The shadows began to lengthen, and the two boys found that they were far from home. They had never been away from the teepee before. Night was coming, and the boys were afraid.

Their fear was increased when they saw that they were being followed by Mato, the Bear. The two boys, not knowing what to do, turned and ran fast. The bear snarled and also ran fast. The bear drew close. The boys knew he would soon be upon them.

In one last effort, the boys cried out to the Mighty

Spirit to help them. They fell to the ground, hoping the bear might pass over them.

Then they felt a trembling beneath them. They raised their heads to see if the bear was shaking them. No, the ground around them was rising toward the sky. They were on the top of a mountain of solid rock. The boys were safe from the jaws of the great bear below, who in his efforts to reach them was tearing great jagged gashes in the sides of the rock with his claws.

To this day Devil's Tower in Wyoming, with its scarred sides and flat top, remains as a token of the Mighty Spirit's kindness to, and watchfulness over, little Sioux children.

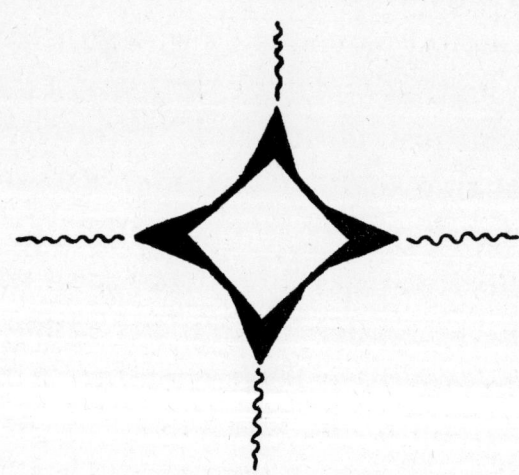

HOW ENEMY SWIM LAKE WAS NAMED

Long ago, before the coming of the white men, the Sisseton Sioux and the Chippewas were rivals for the Lake Region in what is now northeastern South Dakota. The Sioux wanted the country for its buffalo hunting, and the Chippewas liked the wild grapes and plums growing in the thickets around the lakes.

One night a band of Sissetons was camped on a point of land that almost reaches a long, high island in a certain lake. With water on three sides, and a guard watching from a hill behind the camp, there was no fear of enemies attacking without warning. There was much dancing and eating.

Meanwhile a war party of Chippewas from the Father of Waters country was on a hunting trip. One evening they saw the reflection of fire in the sky and followed the light to the lake shore.

The crafty Chippewas were aware of the Sioux customs. They planned a surprise attack on the village after the powwow was over and all were asleep.

The Chippewas hid in the woods across the bay from the island. While the Indians waited, they made rafts from basswood logs lashed together with grapevines. The war party slipped silently to the island on the rafts. They were certain the Sioux would not expect an attack from that side.

While the tom-toms beat loudly in the Sioux camp, the enemy quietly waded across the waist-deep sand bar to the point of land and hid in the bushes.

More wood was needed for the Sioux's fire. Old women were sent to gather firewood. One squaw, walking along the beach picking up driftwood, heard her dog growling. She went to see what was causing the animal to be uneasy.

She came upon a man in strange war paint, crouching low in the bushes. The man hit her with his tomahawk as she screamed. The other women ran to the camp, crying out: "Enemies, enemies!"

The Sisseton chief formed his battle plans quickly. He told the older men to go on horseback around the bay and wait in the woods. He ordered the young warriors to pursue the Chippewas to the nearby island and scalp them all.

Outnumbered, the Chippewas fled to the island, shooting arrows back as they ran. They hid behind trees, but the Sioux braves chased them to the end of the island. The Chippewas had only one chance to escape. They jumped into the lake and started to swim in the darkness across the bay to the woods where they had left their horses.

As the Chippewas reached shore they were met by the older men on horses. Those that were not trampled to death were drowned or tomahawked.

The Sissetons had many enemy scalps. They sang and danced all night. The chief laughed much, saying: "*Tak-niwan, tak-niwan;* the swimming enemy, the swimming enemy."

To this day the lake is known as Enemy Swim Lake, and many arrowheads and tomahawks are found along the shores.

PUNISHED WOMAN'S LAKE

A BAND of Sioux was camped on the banks of a small lake where game and fish were plentiful. They were at peace with the Chippewas, and everyone was happy.

Warriors sat and talked of their deeds in hunting and on the warpath, each one trying to outdo the other. The women were busy scraping hides, gathering wood, and cooking.

Young maidens sewed shells and porcupine quills. Each one sang her dream of a great warrior who would come to her father with gifts, and how she would ride away, the wife of a handsome young brave.

All save We-wa-ke, fairest maiden of the camp. Her heart was given to the young warrior, Wanblee Tonka, or Big Eagle, whose bravery in battle, courage on the hunt, and prowess with the bow and arrow far surpassed the accomplishments of all the other young men of the tribe.

Punished Woman's Lake

Four times in as many moons Big Eagle came to We-wa-ke's father with gifts, only to be refused.

One day came an old chief, White Tail Wolf, bearing presents. Her father accepted them. We-wa-ke begged him not to give his only daughter to this old, feeble chieftain. In spite of her crying, the father gave the pretty maiden to old White Tail Wolf, who dragged her weeping to his lodge.

A great feast was held. While White Tail Wolf smoked at the council fire and bragged of his deeds, Big Eagle stole through the night to We-wa-ke. She ran away with him on his pony.

Old White Tail Wolf, full of food and very tired, turned his footsteps toward his teepee to see his young bride.

The old chief found his teepee empty. He called to all the warriors in the camp. He called on the evil spirit to help find his wife. Big Eagle was also missing; so all the warriors mounted their horses and followed the runaways.

The braves soon returned bearing the two lovers bound with rawhide strips.

The lovers knew that their lives were ending; so they proudly raised their heads, declared their love to each other, and vowed to meet in the happy hunting grounds.

Old White Tail Wolf was so angry he buried his knife in the young warrior's breast. Then he ordered We-wa-ke to be bound to a tree on the shore of the lake. She said she would never be his bride. In his anger he shot an arrow into her heart.

Old White Tail Wolf ordered stones to be placed in the form of a warrior and a maid side by side, as a shameful reminder to all Indians. When he called upon the evil spirit to take them to everlasting sorrow, the Great Spirit heard him. As the bad chief was saying his evil words he was killed by lightning from a clear sky.

Women fled in terror. The braves piled stones on the body of the chief to remind all that he was a murderer and an outcast from the tribe.

The tribe moved westward, never to forget the sorrow upon the shores of what was known from that time on as Punished Woman's Lake.

The stone figures of the chief who had bad thoughts in his heart, and of the two lovers still stand on the banks of the lake near the town of South Shore in eastern South Dakota.

MAIDEN'S ISLE

THERE once lived on the shores of Lake Kampeska a hunter and his beautiful daughter, Minnecotah. The young men of the tribe smiled at her and many of them wanted her for a wife.

But the heart of Minnecotah was turned toward a brave hunter who often visited there. He had journeyed to his home in the Wahpeton country and was not expected to return for several moons.

The young braves of the tribe wished her to choose among them instead of marrying the wandering hunter.

One day when the young men told her to make a choice quickly, Minnecotah said that whoever could throw a stone farthest into the lake would have her love. The men threw pebbles and rocks and big boulders, each trying to outthrow the other. No one could judge which stone had been thrown the farthest because of the waves.

After days of throwing rocks, the young men realized that the wily Minnecotah had played a trick on them and that none could claim the right to marry her.

So many rocks had been thrown that an island of stones had been formed in the lake.

The angry young men seized Minnecotah and put her on the island. There was no food or shelter there. The men were certain she would make a choice as soon as she was hungry enough.

A great white pelican saw Minnecotah and each night the bird brought fish and berries for her to eat. Minnecotah's lover returned. During the night he took her from the island and together they went to his home.

When the young men discovered that Minnecotah was gone, they decided that the white pelican had been sent by the sun god to take her away.

The island of stones can still be seen in Lake Kampeska, near Watertown, South Dakota.

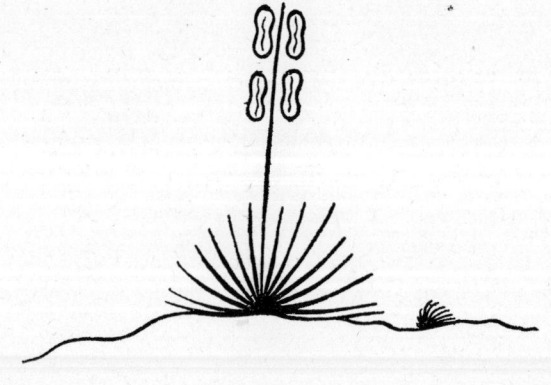

LAKE OF THE BIG LODGE

ONE fall, only a few years before the coming of the white settlers, a band of Sioux Indians was on a hunting trip in the country of the Big Sioux River. Although it was the time of the year to go to their winter camp, the hunters delayed because there were so many buffalo.

Suddenly a great snow fell and the wind was too strong for the Indians to travel. The band was caught in the blizzard on the shores of a large lake. Wood was scarce and there were not enough teepees; so they all put their tents together. Only one fire was needed in the one big lodge, and the people lived there all winter.

In the spring the buffalo hides used in making the lodge were taken away, but the poles were left standing.

Ever since that time the lake has been known as The Standing of the Big Lodge, and its Indian name, Tetonkaha, is still used. The lake is in Brookings County, near Arlington, South Dakota.

THE SACK OF GOLD AT LONG LAKE

This is a story that Indians tell about Gray Foot, a Santee Sioux, who took part in the Indian outbreak of 1862.

Early one morning a band of Santees raided the Government Agency at Martin, Minnesota. The post was guarded by only a few soldiers who were either killed or frightened away. The payroll for the agency had recently arrived and gold coins were piled on a table. The Indians quickly divided the money among them. Gray Foot put his share of money in a flour sack and tied it on the back of his horse. Then the Indians fled westward into Dakota.

Word was sent out by the United States War Department that anyone found with gold coins in his teepee or in his bundles would, by that evidence, be considered guilty of murder. Gray Foot was frightened, so he took

The Sack of Gold at Long Lake 127

his sack of gold to the banks of a lake. Between two straight willows at the east end of the lake Gray Foot buried the flour sack containing his gold coins.

He did not tell anyone about the buried gold for many years, although he was often asked. Then, one day when he was very ill, he called his sons together and told them the secret.

"The sack of gold is buried between two straight willows at the east end of Long Lake," he said. "I have never been there since. It is yours."

The sons looked and looked for the place. There were several lakes known as Long Lake, and around each of them were tree stumps and new trees. Many people have searched for the treasure, but it has never been found.

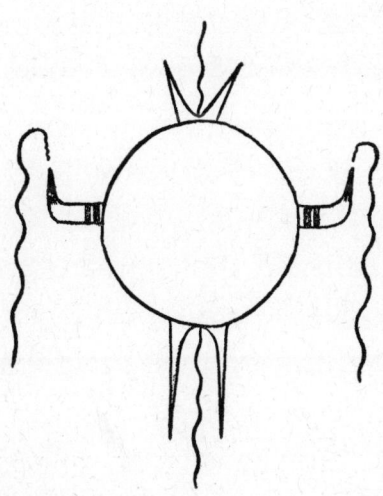

THE STORY OF STANDING ROCK

MANY years ago when the buffalo still roamed the Dakota plains, the people of a Sioux band made camp in a valley of the Missouri River. They were going to pick enough wild fruit for their winter supply.

While they were at this camp a strange changing of a maiden into stone came about. One dark night there was loud talking in the lodge of a chief. The eldest daughter of the chief was being scolded for having told her parents a lie. Telling falsehoods is contrary to the tribe's code and standard of morals.

The chief told the daughter she would have to stay in the teepee until she learned to tell the truth. Instead, she went out into the night, weeping. She walked north towards a towering butte.

The chief thought the daughter wanted to talk with the spirits alone. He told the family to go to bed and await her return.

The Story of Standing Rock

The next morning a strange object was seen on the high butte near the camp. Several braves climbed up the butte and there discovered a pillar of rock resembling a sitting woman. She faced the rising sun.

The daughter of the chief had not returned; so it was believed that the girl had been transformed into a pillar of stone in punishment for her disobedient act.

Ever since this legendary event took place, the Indians have called this place Sitting Woman Rock. In 1873 the United States Government changed the name to Standing Rock, the name which the reservation bears today. The stone is considered to be holy, and it now stands on a pedestal in front of the Standing Rock Agency headquarters at Fort Yates, North Dakota.

HOW SNAKE BUTTE WAS NAMED

At a time when the Arikara Indians were still living along the banks of the Missouri River, a young Arikara brave was hit by the arrow of one of his mortal enemies, the Sioux. Although wounded to the death, the young brave ran a lurching, swaying course as long as he had strength to move. In admiration of his courage and endurance, the Sioux placed a rock on every drop of blood that dripped from him as he ran. And at the center of the long weaving line, they placed the symbol of their

How Snake Butte Was Named

own tribe, the turtle. Thus they paid honor to a brave enemy.

The rocks that were placed on the drops of blood were in the form of a great snake. Along the slopes of a hill near Pierre, South Dakota, known as Snake Butte, the winding line of rocks, all but buried in the earth now, is over a half mile in length.

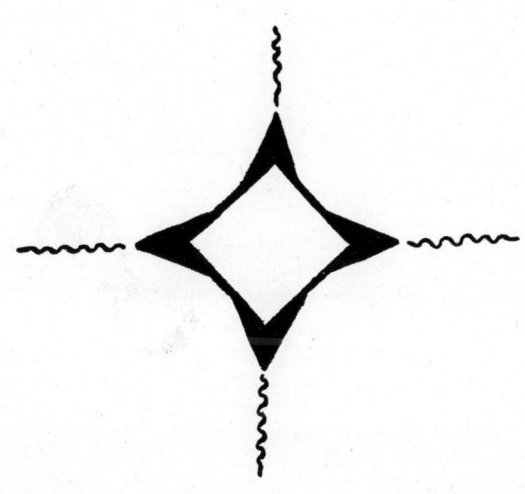

THE NAMING OF WHITE RIVER AND THE BADLANDS

When the Sioux people first visited the bare, lifeless, and sharp hills and the deep, broken cuts in the earth along a river in western Dakota, they said to themselves *"Mako sica,"* which means bad land. Few things grew or lived there, and it was almost impossible to cross the Badlands.

Finally the Indians found a natural opening, now known as Big Foot Pass. This was because Chief Big Foot led his band of four hundred warriors through the Pass in 1890 when the United States soldiers thought that every route was guarded.

It was this same band that went on from the Badlands to the Pine Ridge Reservation. Here Big Foot and his band were killed in the Battle of Wounded Knee, which was the last big fight between the whites and the Indians in the United States.

The Naming of White River and the Badlands

Through the Badlands, which is now a National Monument, flows an unusual river. It rises in Nebraska and crosses the western part of South Dakota to the Missouri River. When the Indians found the river it looked as if it were smoking, for a white fog seems to rise from the valley through which the river flows.

The haze of soft white smoke can often be seen early in the morning, and the Indian name, meaning White Smoke River, has been changed to its present name of White River.

5. Hunting and Battle Stories

A BOY BECOMES A WARRIOR

*I*T has long been the custom for a young Sioux boy to show that he is brave before the older men ask him to ride in the hunt.

This story is about a boy of fourteen who wished to make a name for himself and be known by the braves of his tribe. It seemed to him that the chance would never come.

One day the chief decided that it was time to go on a hunt. He sent out his scouts, who came back with reports of many buffalo at a distance of a ride of one day. As usual the boy was not asked to attend the meeting in the chief's lodge, and this meant that he was to be left behind.

That night when all was still, the boy stole out of camp. He took his own pony from the horse herd, and led it away. On a nearby hill he sat down to wait for the dawn. When the hunters left, he set out on their trail, staying far enough to the rear so as not to be seen.

The herd was sighted and the men moved in among them. The warriors were too busy chasing the buffalo to notice the boy.

The boy picked out a fat buffalo cow on the edge of the herd and charged after it. Because his pony was fleet of foot, it was not long until he was close to the cow. Leaning far over and stringing his bow, he took careful aim and shot. The cow staggered and fell. Leaping from his pony, he drew his knife and cut the cow's throat.

When the others returned to prepare the meat, they found the boy proudly standing beside his kill. When they heard his story and saw that he had made his kill with but one arrow, they gave him much praise. The chief had two men ride ahead into camp, the boy riding beside the chief.

And so that night, with much feasting and dancing, the boy became a warrior.

THE HUNTER RIDES A BUFFALO

A LONE buffalo was feeding on the rich grass which grew on the low ground.

The hunter took good aim with his bow, and wounded the buffalo in the side. In his pain the buffalo charged the horse. The horse, frightened by the sudden attack, stumbled and broke his leg. The angry buffalo then took after the man, trying to ram the hunter with its horns.

The hunter, to save his own life, quickly leaped from the ground to the back of the buffalo. He landed facing to the rear of the buffalo and so he held on to the buffalo's tail. The buffalo roared and jumped, but the hunter held on and pulled hard on the tail.

The buffalo ran in circles until he became exhausted and bled to death from the wound.

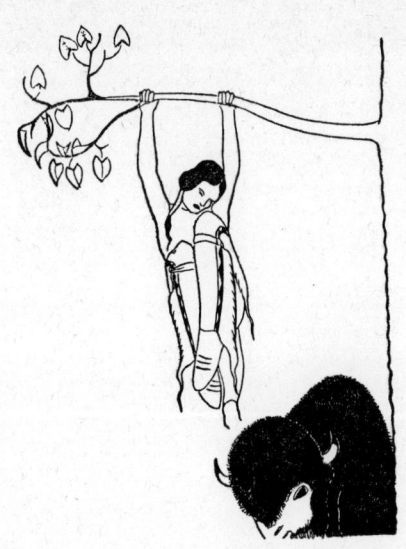

A BUFFALO HUNTER'S ESCAPE

A Sioux hunting party came upon a huge herd of buffalo grazing along a wide draw, and the attack was started with the men divided into two bands.

There was a shout of *"Hoka-He,"* which is like saying, "Let's go," and the horsemen dashed on both sides of the grazing herd.

The sudden attack frightened the herd into running wildly toward the river. Buffalo after buffalo fell wounded or dead from the arrows and gunshot. The other buffaloes ran into the stream and crossed it.

One of the hunters was thrown from his pony, just

as he had shot and wounded a big bull buffalo. He jumped to his feet and raced for the nearest tree with the wounded buffalo close behind him.

The hunter had no time to climb the tree; so he jumped high into the air and got hold of a limb. When the mad buffalo charged, the hunter pulled up his knees. The buffalo brushed the hunter's feet, but the brave hung to the branch. Again the buffalo rushed at the dangling hunter, but the brave raised himself up. The bull missed again.

The brave could hardly hold on to the tree any longer. The buffalo was charging the third time, and this surely would mean the end of the hunter. Then he heard the sound of laughing. It was his brother.

The brother shot at the buffalo just as the buffalo was charging for the man hanging onto the branch. The brother's arrow brought the buffalo down and the hunter fell exhausted from the tree at the same time.

The hunter was always known after as the Man Who Stretched His Arms and Grew Tall.

THE STORY OF THE SCREAMING GHOST

An old warrior who had attained the age of seventy-five winters, and three young braves traveled one day toward a Pawnee village near the Platte River to steal ponies.

The stealing of horses from an enemy tribe had long been a custom with the Sioux. Such a deed was called bravery in those days. These trips were in most cases made on foot. Extra pairs of moccasins were carried along because the stones wore out the buckskin. On this war party, however, the four left the village in such a hurry that they forgot their extra moccasins.

At last, after much travel, they came to a Pawnee village. The four quietly scouted the camp, looking for a time to steal the herd.

Then all of a sudden, an enemy saw them. The old warrior and three young men ran as fast as they could. It was only by many days of hiding behind rocks and running swiftly that they escaped. They soon wore out their moccasins on the stones and rough places.

A camp was made at the foot of a low hill where the braves and the old warrior rested their sore feet. After they had eaten some berries, they began to tell what each one did during the escape.

While they were talking, the old warrior arose and told the others that he was going for a walk to look for food.

Upon his return he told of finding a small lodge on the top of a hill. In it, he said, was a dead Indian. They thought it would be a good idea to pay the dead man a visit, and ask him to give them part of his war shirt to use to mend their moccasins.

Two of the braves eagerly said they would go; but the third brave only closed his eyes and shook his head.

"No, I knew this brave before his sad death. I warn you that he will come to life and run you down no matter how many pipes of peace you smoke for him," he said.

"Well, we must mend our moccasins before we start our trip homeward. I am ready to take a chance," said the old warrior.

"Yes," said one of the younger braves, "the dead man will surely not come to life. I will go."

"So will I," said the third brave.

"Well, you three may go; but as for me, I will walk down toward the stream."

When he reached the river, he quickly took off his leggings and smeared his entire body with mud. Then he took a dried animal skin, which he always carried, and tore out two holes for his eyes. This he drew down over his face. He looked like a ghost or Evil One.

He then ran as fast as he could, hiding behind the hill until he came to the teepee of the dead man. As the three men were nearing the teepee, he pulled up some of the stakes and crawled underneath the covering into it.

The three men sat down in a row a few steps from the teepee, casting their eyes toward the opening of the teepee. The old warrior finally lit the tribal pipe and held it toward the lodge saying, "My esteemed friend, when you were alive you knew the hardships of the warpath. Our clothes and moccasins are worn to shreds. We beg of you—"

At this point his talk ended. The curtain in the doorway moved to one side. What resembled the ghost of the dead Indian looked out fiercely at them.

The pipe dropped from the old warrior's hand. All three of them rose to their feet and with one more look at the moving dead man, they ran like wild deer. In looking back over their shoulders, they discovered that the screaming Evil One was close behind them.

The brave who was slowest was the first victim. A slight touch on his shoulder by the ghost man had a deadly effect and caused the fleeing brave to fall into a faint from fright. The ghost then chased his second victim, touched him, and disposed of him as he had done the first. He then directed his attention to the old warrior who was showing great speed. The ghost chased the old warrior across the river twice, before he finally fell into a faint.

The ghost man then made his way to the river where he took a swim to remove all the mud. He quickly

The Story of the Screaming Ghost 147

dressed himself and returned to the camp. His companions had their heads bound with rawhide strips.

"What does all this mean?" he asked.

But all they would do was groan and gather their belongings for the long trip home without moccasins.

When the brave who had played the trick told the story at a campfire after their return, there was much laughing. And to this day the story of the screaming dead man causes much smiling at campfires and meetings.

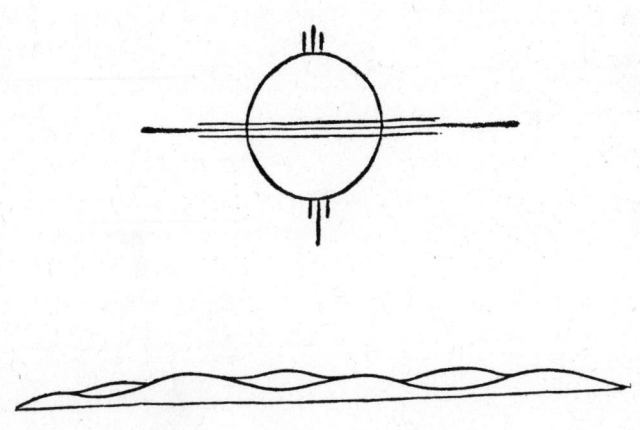

A RUN FOR HIS LIFE

BEFORE there were fences and roads on the Yankton Reservation, the Indians walked across the fields to the Government Agency at Greenwood to get supplies. One day, according to a story the Indians tell, an Indian who was fat and lazy got so hungry that he walked five miles to the agency for a supply of food.

While he was picking out a large order of groceries, he saw a fine-looking hat. It was a military hat like those the white soldiers wore, so he purchased it and put it on. With his sack of supplies thrown over his shoulder, the Indian started for home. As night was coming on, he walked faster than usual for the ground was rough to walk on.

Suddenly he noticed an object directly in front of him. It was getting dark and he could not see what the object before him was, except that it darted and jumped as he walked toward it. He became frightened. No matter in which direction he looked, the object appeared before him. The man walked faster and faster, but the object continued to bob and dance before him.

The Indian knew something was wrong, so he tried to go around. There was no use. When he looked back the object was still there. Then he set out at full speed, zigzagging and stumbling as he ran. He raced through bushes and undergrowth, but still the object was always before him.

The Indian thought this must surely be his end when, finally, he saw the light of his lodge ahead. With one last desperate effort to escape his pursuer, the man dashed on and fell, exhausted, at the doorway. He was battered and bruised from the heavy sack of supplies that had been swinging on his back as he ran.

After being carried in and rested, the man told his story of the chase and boasted of how he had run so fast. The object had disappeared.

The next day when the Indian went outdoors he put on his new hat. It was then that he saw that the demon object had been the heavy hat cord hanging over the brim of his hat in front.

THE BATTALION OF DEATH

There once was an association of the most active and brave young men of the Yankton tribe of the Sioux.

These men, ranging from the ages of thirty to thirty-five years, were bound by a promise never to retreat in the face of danger, never to give way to their enemies, and never to turn to one side. They camped and danced by themselves, apart from the rest of the tribe.

In battle they went forward without sheltering themselves behind trees or other protection.

This promise not to be turned from their course caused disaster on one occasion when the Yanktons were crossing the Missouri River on the ice. Immediately in their path lay a hole, which they might easily have gone around. But the leader went straight forward and was lost. The others attempted to follow his example, but were held back by the rest of the tribe.

The courage of these men was so honored that their place in council was superior even to that of the Chief. But, as may be seen, the carrying out of their promise at all times would have led to the death of the entire band.

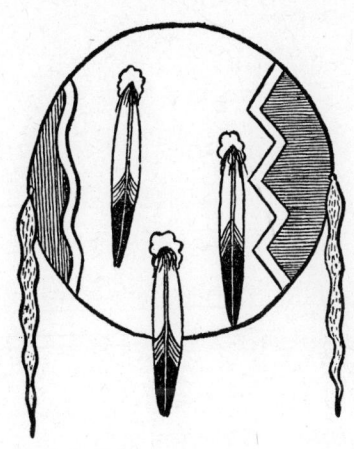

THE SCOUT WHO STOPPED A WAR

When the United States Army established Fort Sisseton after the Indian outbreaks of 1862, Indians were hired as scouts. Old Indians of the Sisseton Reservation in northeastern South Dakota like to recall the days when their fathers were scouts at the fort. Around Sam Brown, the son of a white trader and his Indian wife, has grown a legend of a scout who performed a remarkable feat.

One day in the early spring of 1866, officers at Fort Sisseton learned that a band of Indians was moving south along the James River from near Jamestown to make raids on the settlers. Sam Brown was chief of the Indian scouts, so he was sent to the Ruilliard Trading Post to warn the people there.

A large tribe was living on the Elm River near Ruilliard's, which was about ten miles from the present city of Aberdeen, and Brown had been ordered to try to persuade the tribe not to join in the fighting. The Indian scout left Fort Sisseton near sundown and rode hard, covering the distance of about 55 miles during the night.

At Ruilliard's, Brown was told that Indian carriers had brought word that the President of the United States had signed a treaty that was to stop soldiers from fighting the Indians. The government mailmen serving Fort Sisseton were not as swift as the Indian carriers. Brown realized that the troops at Fort Sisseton planned to leave that very morning to meet the Indians on the James River. He knew he must stop the soldiers before another Indian war was started.

He traded horses with Ruilliard and, with only a little rest, started back to the fort. He had gone only a little way when it began to snow and the wind turned cold. A blizzard swept the prairie and forced him to travel eastward more than north against the stiff, cutting wind. At daybreak he found himself among the Waubay Lakes, far south of the fort. He turned his horse into the wind and rode hard into the storm.

Brown reached the fort in time to stop the troops. He had ridden almost steadily over 130 miles. He was so cold that he could not move his legs; the soldiers had to lift him off his horse.

Sam Brown never moved his legs again. He remained paralyzed all his life as the result of his ride to stop a war.

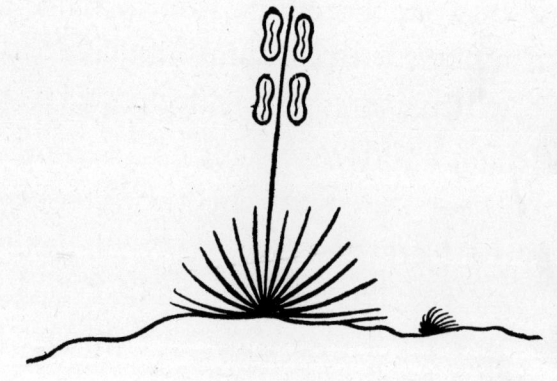

THE FOOL SOLDIERS BAND

The story of the Fool Soldiers Band is a true one, and the Sioux people are very proud to tell it again and again.

Soon after Dakota Territory was formed, a band of Santees went on the warpath and attacked the town of Shetek Lake, Minnesota. They kidnapped two white women and seven children, taking them to the Missouri River. Word that the white people were being held captive came to Fort Pierre.

There a group of young Indian men, known as the Fool Soldier Band because they had promised to help the whites, set out to rescue the women and children. Martin Charger, a brave young Sioux whose grandfather had been a famous white explorer, led the band which included the following men: Kills Game And Comes Back, Strikes Fire, Red Dog, Charging Dog,

One Rib, Swift Bird, Four Bear, Mad Bear, Pretty Bear, and Sitting Bear.

They found the camp of the bad Santees where Grand River joins the Missouri River. The Fool Soldiers asked to trade their horses, food, guns, and clothes for the white people. At last a trade was made and the white women and children were given to the young Indians. As the Fool Soldiers Band had traded all their belongings except one horse, they made a basket for the children to ride in. One woman, who had been shot in the foot, and the basket of children were placed on the one horse. The other woman had no shoes, so Martin Charger gave her his moccasins.

The Fool Soldiers Band delivered the women and children safely to their families. At Mobridge there is a monument to these men.

SITTING BULL'S DANCING HORSE

When the Sioux tribes were moved to reservations, Sitting Bull, the famous medicine man and chief, made his home on the Standing Rock Reservation. Sitting Bull had traveled with Buffalo Bill's Wild West Show for a time, and when he came to live near the Indian village of Little Eagle, South Dakota, he brought with him a trick circus horse.

One day the superintendent of the reservation heard that Sitting Bull was planning to leave. Although Sitting Bull was respected, he was also feared. The superintendent thought that Sitting Bull might start trouble, so 43 Indian police were sent to arrest the chief. The policemen, commanded by Lieutenant Bullhead, who disliked Sitting Bull, arrived at the camp at daybreak, December 15, 1890. They awoke Sitting Bull and dragged him outside. He said he would go peacefully.

A wife was sent to bring him his favorite horse to ride—the circus horse.

Catch-the-Bear, a good friend of Sitting Bull, became angry with Bullhead for arresting the chief. A fight started. Sitting Bull, who was unarmed, was shot in the back and fell dead. A terrific battle followed—Indians against Indians.

When the first shots were fired the circus horse, thinking it was back in the Wild West Show, began doing its tricks. It sat calmly near Sitting Bull and lifted one hoof, then danced around on its hind feet. When the Indians saw the large gray horse performing, they thought it was being guided by the spirit of Sitting Bull and they were very frightened. Many ran away to hide.

When the fighting was over it was found that the old circus horse did not have a single wound, although it had been in the line of fire.